Memories of Keighley

Foreword

Memories of Keighley is a compilation of photographs from the not-too-distant past, chosen according to their ability to rekindle memories of days gone by. The book deliberately concentrates upon a relatively recent period in the town's history, a time which should be within the memory of many readers, and a time which saw massive changes occur in the centre of Keighley with the redevelopment of the local shopping centre.

In compiling the book our objective has been to present the photographs and captions in an entertaining and informative way. *Memories of Keighley* has, in fact got far more to do with entertainment than serious study, but we hope that it is none the worse for that!

Many well-known streets are featured on the following pages, several of which disappeared under the new shopping centres and buildings created in the development of the 1960s and 1970s. The old shops, market area, bus station and cinemas all find a place here, evoking memories of the sights, sounds and even smells of Keighley in the days when we were all a little younger.

Keighley is, in appearance at least, very different to the town featured in the following pages. In common with most other towns in the '60s and '70s, Keighley took steps to improve her shopping centre, with particular regard to car parking, public transport and the increasing demands of national retail chains. The age of concrete, cars and bingo would change the face of Keighley forever. This book has been a pleasure to compile. Whatever your age, we hope you enjoy reading it. Happy memories!

Phil Holland and **Mark Smith**
True North Books.

The draughty but much-loved market area pictured shortly before it was demolished. Crowds flocked to see the opening of the new market in June 1971 by the Mayor, Ald. Sydney Bancroft.

a true north book

Copyright © True North Holdings
ISBN: 1 900 463 01 6

All rights reserved. No part of this publication may be reproduced, stored in a retrieval system or transmitted in any form without the prior written permission of the publishers.

First published in 1997 by:
True North Books
Dean Clough
Halifax
HX3 5AX
Tel 01422 344344
Printed by Joseph Ward ColourPrint
Dewsbury

Memories of Keighley

Contents

Section one	Events & occasions
Section two	At your leisure
Section three	Working life
Section four	Around the town centre
Section five	Wheels of time
Section six	Shopping
Section seven	Bird's eye view

Acknowledgments

The publishers would like to thank the following for helping to make this book possible: Pauline Barfield and the staff of Keighley Library, who kindly allowed us to reproduce a number of photographs from their excellent collection and Ian Dewhirst, the well-known local historian, who supplied a number of pictures as well as a great deal of help with the captions. Thanks are also due to the many local businesses and other organisations who have allowed us to relate their often fascinating histories through the pages of the book. Finally, thanks are also due to Andrew Hales, who organised the local business content of the book and Mandy Walker, who supplied the design flair in abundance.

The closing down sale at Direct Stores attracted hundreds of people in long queues after an announcement was made in the *Keighley News*. Closure of the popular store was brought about by the demolition of properties in the area to make way for the new shopping development. Cooke Lane is famous as the place where Timothy Taylor first established his brewing business in 1858.

Events & special occasions

The Albion Cycling Club treated these children from Aireworth, Starkie, Moss and Bengal Streets to a day trip to Morecambe in 1938. The photograph also illustrates the amenities of Keighley's pre-war railway station, with its toilets, refreshment room and separate waiting accommodation for first and third class passengers. It is a sobering thought to consider how the lives of these children would change, a little over a year later, with the outbreak of the Second World War. Keighley escaped the devastating bomb damage that wrecked the townscape in areas just a few miles away but the rationing, war work and disruption to family life was as much in evidence here as anywhere.

Memories of Keighley

Left: Queen Elizabeth visiting the Royal Ordnance Factory at Steeton in March 1942. For security reasons details were restricted at the time, the Keighley news could only mention the royal visit to a "north eastern factory". The King and Queen spent much of the War making morale-boosting visits to towns and cities throughout the country. The smiling faces in this picture provide an indication of the tremendous affection that was shown to the couple when they visited Keighley.

Popularly known as "The Dump", the Royal Ordnance Factory started production early in 1941 and closed down in August 1945. It produced 204 million munitions components, including 43 million shells and 120 million 20mm shell cases. At its peak over 4000 people were employed at the factory. Workers were brought in by special trains and buses from 62 towns and villages as far apart as Bradford, Nelson and Barnoldswick.

Right: During September and October 1940, British aircraft losses were replaced through the efforts of a Spitfire-Hurricane Fund. In two months Keighley's contribution totalled more than £11,600. As with other fund-raising activities of the time, there was no shortage of innovative ideas from all sections of the community, including children as we can see here. This lively stall was organised by a group of Stockbridge children who sold unwanted household items donated by local residents. They managed to raise the very respectable sum of £8. 7s.

1940 saw the introduction of bacon, butter and sugar rationing in Britain. The same year Winston Churchill became Prime Minister after the resignation of Chamberlain. This was also the year that the Home Guard was formed, and a third of a million troops were evacuated from Dunkirk in May. Aircraft were never far from people's thoughts at the time this picture was taken. The R.A.F began the night bombing of Germany and scores of German planes were shot down each day as they made their unwelcome visits to the cities of Britain.

Memories of Keighley

Right: Her Royal Highness the Princess Royal walking along North Street with Mayor Tom Snowden on May 9 1943. Her visit was the highlight of Wings for Victory Week, during which Keighley raised £1,453,147 for the war effort. It is difficult to imagine the thoughts going through the minds of the people who turned out to see the royal visitor; in 1943, after four long years of war, local people would grasp any opportunity for a celebration, and a glimpse of 'royalty' would provide welcome cheer.

Increasingly, at this time, the War was beginning to go the way of the Allies in 1943. The Eighth Army reached Tripoli and the R.A.F began to bomb Berlin. It was the year that Italy declared war on Germany and the Allied army in North Africa was placed under the command of Eisenhower.

The around-the-clock bombing of Germany began in 1943, part of the process of softening-up the enemy before the final onslaught.

Left: Another example of the contribution made by children to the Spitfire-Hurricane fund-raising in 1940, some being photographed presenting their contributions to Mayor J.W Wardle who had initiated the fund locally. Here is young Thelma Wright handing over £5 5s. which she had raised by selling scent bags. Publicity was a key factor in maintaining morale and ensuring that the efforts of local fundraisers was recognised. This would also add weight to future money-spinning activities, of which there was an endless stream during the war years. Throughout the war local newspapers 'kept score' on how much had been saved and salvaged, and reports of the progress made by each section of the community were published weekly.

Memories of Keighley

Right: Town Hall Square was the venue for a parade made up of various military and public service personnel who were keenly listening to an address by Rear Admiral Dennis Boyd, Fifth Sea Lord and head of the Fleet Air Arm, at the start of Wings for Victory Week in 1943. The Town Hall Square was packed to capacity to hear how important Britain's need for aircraft was in the war against the Nazis. By the end of the fund raising week, which saw keen competition from virtually every town in Great Britain, Keighley would have raised the amazing sum of £1.4 million. Towns were 'judged' by how much money was raised per head of the population, and this was measured on a regional basis. Keighley's efforts were compared to the rest of the West Riding of Yorkshire and the small town of Ripponden took the award.

Left: The "stand-down" parade of the Keighley (27th West Riding) Battalion of the Home Guard on a dismal Sunday afternoon early in December, 1944. This is D Company, commanded by Major Norman Feather, who had won the Military Cross during the First World War. The salute was taken along North Street in front of a small podium upon which Colonel Sir Donald Horsfall, the Deputy Section Commander, was standing. By the time this picture was taken Keighley had endured five long years of war, with all the worry and restrictions which went with it.

Memories of Keighley

Left: The end of the Second World War in August 1945 was celebrated in every locality with "V.J" (victory over Japan) parties. The 'Keighley News' commented that "the tea and supper parties arranged in gardens, backyards, streets and around bonfires" were "too numerous to mention". Typical fare at such al fresco gatherings comprised "sandwiches, veal, potted meat, custards, jellies, blanc-mange and cakes and buns". There was a craze for icing cakes in red, white and blue, with table cloths to match. Here, in an informal snapshot, are residents of Rosslyn Grove, Haworth.

Below left: An open-air party at Thwaites on Sunday, August 19th 1945. Like many similar scenes, it was taken by George A Shore, a prolific freelance photographer who also ran Shore's Warehouse at the bottom of Keighley Market, selling linoleum and carpet squares. The number 32 jotted towards the bottom right-hand corner indicates that he had photographed at least 31 other street parties.

Below: The women and children attending this Victory party for the Malsis Road area on August 18, 1945, were allowed to use the forecourt of Lund Park Methodist Church which provided an ideal setting for this street party group photograph.

Memories of Keighley

Glorious sunshine met HRH Princess Anne when she visited Keighley in June 1977 as part of her tour marking the Queen's silver jubilee. The princess arrived in Keighley by helicopter, landing in the grounds of the Holy Family School to be met by Mr. John N. Smallwood, chairman of the area Silver Jubilee Committee. Thousands of supporters lined her route to Cliffe Castle on the bright summer's day to watch and cheer as the royal motorcade sped by. The Princess wore a powder blue fitted coat and pill box hat with an unusual scarf effect flowing down past the neck. During her walkabout at Cliffe Castle, the princess watched various demonstrations by local children and chatted with them in a warm and relaxed manner. Princess Anne joined children from Utley School in their centenary celebrations, before travelling back to her helicopter at the end of the tour. Everyone agreed that the occasion had been a resounding success and that the people of Keighley could be proud of the impression local children had made on the royal visitor.

At your leisure

Left Children of Worth Village Primary School prepare to dance around a maypole. The picture dates from about 1940. Note the simple choreographic guidelines which have been chalked on the floor.

The children's mothers had all made a special effort to turn them out smartly, judging by the clean white shoes and ribbons in the girls' hair. The children in the picture appear to be aged around six or seven years, so most would now be in their early to mid sixties at the time of writing. They would have witnessed some of the most dynamic years in the history of the world during their lives.

What stories they could tell us now, of the changes that transformed their town, in terms of shopping, housing, transport and the world of work. Their childhood memories will be coloured by the war; memories of queues and rationing, of air raid shelters and the loss of loved-ones, the emotional highs and lows over a six year period that shaped their lives and personalities forever. God bless them all!

Right: During the 1930s, children of Keighley's new Guard House Estate were treated to an annual trip. This is the first, on May 24th, 1930. It was organised by Guard House Social and Welfare Committee and paid for by by County Alderman J.J Brigg, whose family had sold the site to Keighley Corporation for housing development. 200 grateful children travelled to Malham in the Yorkshire Dales aboard five West Yorkshire Road Car Company 'buses, where they "raided the sweet shops", walked en-masse to Malham Cove and had tea at the Airedale Private Hotel.

Most of the little lads featured in the picture - and, no doubt some of the girls too would have been excited by the news that Amy Johnson had succeeded in flying 'solo' from London to Sydney - in less than 20 days.

Memories of Keighley

Left: By November of 1935, in an era which enjoyed dancing and socialising in formal dress, the annual ball of the Keighley Inland Revenue staff was being described as "one of the most important dances of the season". That year some 220 guests danced to the music of Rowland Powell and his Ten Rhythm Aces from Leeds. Proceeds were donated to the Keighley Victoria Hospital.
1935 saw the launch of the popular musical "Porgy and Bess" by Gershwin in New York. At the cinema the latest block busters were "Mutiny on the Bounty" and "Anna Karenina". In the dance halls the latest craze was the Rumba.
Popular songs from the time included "Begin the Beguine"; "The Music Goes Round and Round"; "I got plenty o' Nuthin"; "It Ain't Necessarily So" and "Just One of Those Things".

Right: Keighley Police No.1 and No.2 tug of war teams in action during a "Stay at Home" Parish Feast in 1942 when sports and entertainments were laid on in an attempt to dissuade holidaymakers from wartime travelling. Tremendous efforts were made to reduce wastage during the war, and to re-use or recycle ordinary household products where possible. Railings were torn up, old pots and pans were handed in (the latter being particularly useful in the production of light weight aircraft parts). Indeed, anything that could be melted down and turned into a machine or device to aid the *war effort* was eagerly snapped up by the authorities.

Memories of Keighley

Right: An imposing view of one of Keighley's all-time favourite entertainment venues. Opened in 1900 as the Queen's Theatre, it was re-named 'The Hippodrome' less than a decade later. The Theatre was known by both names by local people throughout its sixty year life. Over the years the top names in music hall entertainment appeared here - Gracie Fields, Tommy Handley and George Formby to name but a few. This photograph dates from 1956, the year that the Theatre closed. The fine old building was pulled down in 1961 as one of the early moves in the redevelopment of Keighley's town centre. It had been the subject of a compulsory purchase order by the Corporation, the land and building being acquired for less than £20,000. During the redevelopment of the town centre there were several disputes about the compulsory purchase of shops, houses and offices; several of these were settled in widely-reported court cases.

Left: A deserted view of North Street featuring the *Essoldo* Cinema, recorded in June 1966. The street scene is unusually quiet, save for one or two passers-by outside the local newspaper offices. There were many well-known shops along this section of North Street at the time this photograph was taken; Tindall's the butchers, Emmott Brothers the builders' merchants and A.E Barrett's to name just a few which operated from the lock-up premises. The age of television and bingo had done severe damage to the trade enjoyed by local cinemas, not just in Keighley, but in every town in the country. By the mid-1960s Keighley had just two remaining cinemas, the Essoldo and the Ritz, after losing six similar establishments in the space of just eight years. The Ritz, interestingly, was also situated along North Street. Further along the street are the offices of the 'Keighley News' the location of the newspaper since 1928, though the building has been extensively enlarged and eventually rebuilt over the years that followed.

Memories of Keighley

Left: The Keighley Vocal Union in 1960, with the five trophies they won that October at the Blackpool Music Festival. Seated in the centre of the front row are president T. Anderson, conductor Jack Smith, and Frank Haygarth, the then only founder-member and original secretary in 1906. "You bring a poetic magic to your vivid tone", Blackpool judges had said of their singing of 'Hymn to Music', "and the result is sheer wonder." Nineteen-sixty was also the year that Lionel Bart's popular musical "Oliver" was launched and the "Twist" took nightclubs and dance halls by storm.

Right: The owner of this three-wheeled *Morgan Super* sportscar, photographed at Spencer Street in 1946, was Bernard Lee, son of Keighley's N.S.P.C.C. Inspector. The background includes several post-war details: the small boy on the left with his toy trolley; the corner shop with its big tin advertisement for Brooke Bond Tea, and the sliding curtain on the outside of the door of the right-hand house positioned to protect the paint work in hot weather.

These small three-wheeled cars may seem odd to the younger motorists of the modern age, but in terms of fuel economy and the efficient use of resources used in their construction, not to mention pure driving exhilaration, they were difficult to beat!

Memories of Keighley

For many years Fred's Ices were a familiar feature of Keighley Gala processions. Fred Greenwood had opened a Fell Lane grocery store and off-licence in 1928, subsequently making his own ice cream. In 1936 the Keighley Friendly societies' Gala programme contained the following advertisement:

"To celebrate our London success we shall distribute during the procession 1000 tasting samples (Free) so you may test the quality which gained us the The Grand Diploma of Merit at Crystal Palace, London, February 1936. Competition was open to all countries. Fred's Fell Lane."

For years thereafter it was Fred's custom to throw tubs of ice cream from his van into the crowds of enthusiastic spectators along the route of the gala procession. In this photograph, bystanders in the foreground have their hands outstretched in the hope of catching one.

Memories of Keighley

No book on Keighley would be complete without a mention of the splendid work which has been carried out by the Keighley and Worth Valley Railway Preservation Society. This photograph dates from August 1962 and features enthusiastic activity underway at the Haworth Railway Station. This was to be the base of the Society between 1962 and 1968 when it was rented from British Railways. The Society was founded at a public meeting in March 1962 with the main aim of preserving the Worth Valley Railway as a going concern. The last scheduled passenger service to run on the line had been in December 1961, though a daily goods train ran for a while longer than that. Re-opening the line to the public was to prove a challenging task for the members of the Society, but their determination and sense of purpose saw them through.

Working life

A rare and unusual view of the inside of a gas holder at Thwaites. It was captured in July 1914, around forty years after the facility was first opened. The gas holder, when completed, had a capacity of 750,000 cubic feet, a fact graphically illustrated in the summer of 1930 when one of the holders blew up in a spectacular explosion. Keighley's gas supplies, unlike the supplies to most other towns, has always been in public control. In the earliest days charges were based upon the number of jets the householder or business had in their premises. The fee was just over £1 per jet, per year. Interestingly, the supply was cut off at 10 pm each night and not available between mid-May and mid-September each year!

Memories of Keighley

Every town in wartime Britain was faced with raising money for the war effort in the years between 1939 and 1945. Keighley was no exception, and her citizens responded by buying huge amounts of National Savings Certificates, War Bonds, and Defence Bonds. In addition there were specific campaigns to raise funds to buy tanks, warships and aircraft. Keighley's Warship Week took place in March 1942 with an initial target of £700,000 to buy the destroyer HMS Marne. The actual figure was, quite incredibly, almost doubled by the end of the week at £1,320,000. Attempts were later made to increase the total to £1.4 million so that a 'mate for Marne' could be purchased. War Weapons Week had earlier seen Keighley people raise £1,044,105, a staggering £18 per head for the war effort.

Throughout the War Keighley's fund-raising activity was co-ordinated by The Keighley Savings League, an progress was reported through the pages of the Keighley News virtually every week. This photograph shows the product of another fund raising campaign to buy a Spitfire. It was taken in October 1940. The Spitfire Fund had a target of £10,000, but this was surpassed and the total eventually reached £11,600.

Thousands of people gave generously in Keighley and District and their efforts were acknowledged by Lord Beaverbrook, Minister for Aircraft Production in a letter to the Mayor. It was decided that the surplus in the Spitfire appeal should be donated to the RAF Benevolent Fund.

A £5,000 donation from the Keighley firm Dean, Smith and Grace of Valley Tool Works resulted in another fighter being purchased and named the 'Dean, Smith and Grace Spitfire'.

Memories of Keighley

Left: A charming scene from 1962 showing part of a ward and some of the new mums in the new maternity block. 1962 saw the introduction of a relaxation and mothercraft class at the hospital which was quite advanced for the time. The course lasted 12 weeks and was unique in as much as it was run by a physiotherapist, a midwife and a health visitor. These were changing times in the field of maternity care and childbirth; mothers were gradually moving away from the tradition of giving birth at home, and those choosing to have their baby in hospital were staying there for a shorter period - typically five days instead of the usual ten. There was more emphasis in care at home after the birth, with home visits by health visitors being the norm.

Reports of the Board of Health make interesting reading; there was concern about the first death in the area from diphtheria since 1947. Better news was that road deaths had fallen to five for the whole of 1962 from 12 during the previous year. Over the previous 6 years a total of 1000 slums had been cleared in Keighley and the standard of housing was beginning to rise. This was to make one of the largest contributions to the improving health of local people over the coming decade.

Left: This scene, dating from November 1961 depicts a fire drill taking place in the Braithwaite area of Keighley. The delightful fire appliance seen here would have acted like a magnet to scores of local children eager to get a rare close-up view of the vehicle and the heroic dark-suited firemen who looked after her. The bright red, hand-crafted coachwork and brilliant deep chrome bells and fittings made the engines popular with every little boy. At the time this picture was taken the Fire Station was situated at Coney Lane, and the accommodation and facilities there left much to be desired for the modern fire fighting force. By July 1964 a new Fire Station had been opened on Bradford Road. The new building could house six appliances in the 90ft vehicle bay and had a 65ft drill tower.

Memories of Keighley

Working on the buses used to be a family affair. Employees at the Keighley depot of the West Yorkshire Road Car Company Ltd. included a dozen married couples, plus a number of sons and daughters, brothers and sisters. This group of drivers, conductors, conductresses and office staff photographed in 1952, shows some of them. **Back row, left to right:** Miss J. Brown, Driver C. Stone, Mrs C. Stone, Mrs D. Judson, Conductor W.O. Watson, Miss M.Hartley, Mrs M Hartley, Driver W. Hartley, Mrs I. Hollingdrake, Driver T. Hollingdrake, Mrs C. Holmes, Mrs E. Maris. **Front row:** Driver A. Judson, Conductor T. Brechany, Mrs J. Brechany, Mrs M. Manterfield, Driver G. Manterfield, Mrs B. Firth and Miss E. Hartley.

Memories of Keighley

DSG Lathes, part of Keighley's proud engineering heritage.

Better known today as DSG Lathes, the company began life in 1865 as Dean, Smith and Grace, the named gentlemen being debts had been paid off by 1883 and the firm's reputation was growing. In 1898 the partnership became a limited company. Reorganisation and rebuilding took place and it was decided that the firm would specialise in the lathe, although, during the first World War, breech blocks for guns were made too.

The business continued to prosper between the wars and afterwards. From 1938 affairs were run by Sir Harry Smith, James Pearson Smith and Mr. Bert Laycock. More property was acquired and, after the directors had visited the USA, more plant was purchased from there.

In 1948 the prototype of a new range of lathes was exhibited at Olympia which resulted in fame for the firm in London and also in Toronto and led to considerable trade with Canada Between 1962 and 1965, the Nelson Works, the new foundry in Lawkholme Lane, was built and opened, complete with the latest equipment. There the new centre lathe was produced that was exhibited at Olympia in 1964.

In 1974, the company was sold to Monarch Machine Tool Company of the USA. Demand grew in the 1970s and 1980s for Monarch's CNC lathes, so that they survived competition from Japan. The present company, DSG Lathes was formed in 1992 after Monarch decided to withdraw from the UK market. DSG specialises in producing lathes to suit individual customers' requirements and their order books are filling satisfactorily.

Above: A letterhead dating from 1914. **Far left:** *The cover of a catalogue which was issued in 1889. Inside the book were wonderful line drawings of the machinery offered by DSG.* **Left:** *An early line drawing of a milling machine, made by Dean, Smith & Grace and illustrated in their 1889 catalogue.*

Keighley engineers who borrowed money to buy land from the Duke of Devonshire on which to build a foundry. It was a single-storey machine shop of 3,000 square feet and, when business began, every penny was ploughed back into it.

With more than 150 staff working a 54 hour week, all

DSG Lathes Limited

PO Box 15, Pitt Street, Keighley BD21 4PG
Telephone: 01535 605261
Fax: 01535 680921

Memories of Keighley

Local family firm with three-quarters-of-a-century of printing heritage

A small attic room in Haworth main street was the first premises of the company that Walter Parker set up in 1914. As soon as his work was under way it had to be abandoned as Mr Parker served his country in the Great War.

The Keighley Gazette

By 1926 business had restarted and flourished. New premises were needed - and found in Low Street in the centre of Keighley. Here Walter had the old Keighley Gazette printed - a local newspaper with a 15,000 copy print run on a hand-fed press, with all the newsprint being carried upstairs without the luxury of a goods lift! Activities were trimmed back during the Depression but the company soon fought back to prosperity. It became Walter Parker (Keighley) Ltd in 1943 with directors Jack and Alan Parker and Jack Briggs joining Walter.

Wellington Street

In the 50s and 60s, now trading in Wellington Street, the firm gradually introduced automated monotype and linotype. There was so much work that it was difficult to find enough workers! In 1961 came another move - to former Sunday School premises in West Lane. The company consolidated its reputation here.

New equipment arriving at the factory on Wellington Street during the 1950s.

Typesetting and page make-up the 'old way'.

Memories of Keighley

The new factory in Royd Way, Keighley.

Change of leadership

When managing director Jack Parker decided to retire, the new regime was ready for a new approach. The Parker family sold the business to Dennis and Nina Russell. Thelma Shackleton, the Company Secretary stayed on - she was the common denominator. The company adopted the latest process, offset litho in an attempt to become the best colour printers in Yorkshire.

A further move became necessary, this time to the Sheetfed market. Expensive offset litho printing presses were installed, a gamble that soon paid off.

A final move to Royd Ings Works, a modern industrial site, gave good access to the railway and motorway, and provided a roomier environment for the workers. As the company grew and invested in new colour technology it was decided in 1985 to change its name to Coltec Parker. Now it produces work for major national companies.

In 1997 £350,000 was invested in the firm, providing the equipment needed to expand services to the Direct Mail industry. By the millennium Coltec Parker will look back on over three-quarters-of-a-century as a family company and forward to greater things.

The Parker family admiring some new equipment.

Memories of Keighley

Fifty years of progress at Peter Black - one of Keighley's best known businesses

Most Keighley folk will be familiar with the successful company known locally as 'Peter Blacks'. Peter Black Holdings plc, as it is more properly known, has developed rapidly over the last 50 years and is now a major contender in several important markets, including footwear and accessories, toiletries, cosmetics, skincare, healthcare and distribution. The company is proud to supply some of the most respected people in the world of retailing, including Marks and Spencer, with which it has had a strong relationship for many decades.

Strong views

The story behind Peter Black can be traced back to 1947 when Mr Peter Black took over a small Keighley-based manufacturer of bags and webbing products. Peter Black had very clear and strong views about how to organise and run his business, his philosophy being "work hard, aim at perfection, organise every detail, keep your team happy, alert and well informed".

The approach obviously worked, as the company grew quickly and established an increasing reputation for producing the highest standards of quality and, most importantly, on-time delivery.

The success achieved in those post-war years enabled the company to grow and expand the range of products offered. For many years the traditional ranges still played an important role in the firm's activities, and by 1960 this was reflected in the impressive sales figures achieved for these lines, with over one million shopping and travel bags and more than two million pairs of slippers being sold.

Family links

Today the traditional values and company ethos established by the founder, Peter Black, are as strong as ever, and the family link is maintained by the Chairman, Gordon Black, son of the founder. Visitors to the

Memories of Keighley

business operates from 11 locations throughout the U.K, each equipped to the highest standards in their respective fields. Computerised information systems and efficient physical distribution ensure that products are quickly delivered to the marketplace.

'People' continue to be regarded as the company's most valuable asset, and over 1400 staff are engaged in the firm's activities. Everyone at Peter Black is aware of the need to stay 'one step ahead' of the competition in some very challenging markets. The business may be bigger, the procedures more sophisticated and dynamic, but the pursuit of quality remains the primary objective.

Facing page: The early days of Peter Black. Even then the huge amount of orders was evident, although the mode of transport was vastly different to the swish articulated lorries that are a common sight on our motorways today (see below). **Left:** *Workers just after the second world war; sewing handbags. Singer sewing machines are doing their usual sterling service. The workforce chose their own hairstyles and were free to wear their own clothes. This, of course, was in the days before Government safety regulations dictated such matters.*

Keighley operation are impressed by the strong sense of teamwork that pervades the organisation, a characteristic of the firm which has existed for half a century. The company is proud of its roots and its heritage, but that does not mean it is backward looking. Peter Black competes in some of the toughest markets in the world and relies upon superior levels of innovation, design and customer service for its continued success. Four major markets are involved; Footwear & Accessories, Toiletries & Cosmetics, Healthcare and Distribution. In all, the

Memories of Keighley

Bethel Rhodes; the visionary genius behind Keighley's master wireworkers

Mr Bethel Rhodes was a remarkable figure in the Victorian era, the period during which he made his most notable achievements. His father was a successful businessman who had been running a busy and thriving wireworking concern in the Bradford area. Mr. Rhodes was born in Shelf in 1847 and began working for his father at the age of ten. At fourteen he was receiving the princely sum of 2s. 6d. per week for his labours, plus, of course, a wealth of priceless knowledge and expertise which would stand him in good stead for the rest of his business career.

The early days

The now well-known Keighley connection almost failed to happen; Bethel Rhodes' father wanted his son to establish a branch of his business in Newcastle, at a distance of over 100 miles and an arduous and time consuming journey at the time. Bethel Rhodes was far from keen on the idea, influenced, perhaps, by his decision to marry a local girl at the age of 19. A compromise was reached and Bethel moved instead to nearby Keighley to set up a wiremaking business at the premises on Coney Lane. By 1886 business was doing well enough to take

Memories of Keighley

Facing page: main picture: The animals of Sanger's Circus parade along North Street in 1902. The sign on the far right of the picture: Rhodes Wireworks points to the location of Bethel Rhodes premises. The site was later to be occupied by the Town Hall. **Left:** *An early line drawing of the Rhodes Wireworks on North Street.* **Below:** *Founder of the business, Mr Bethel Rhodes. The various line drawings of wire products are reproduced from a turn-of-the-century catalogue. They are (left to right) wire hanging basket, round brush and straight mesh riddle.*

larger premises in North Street, on a site later to be occupied by the Town Hall. A variety of products were on offer during these early days of the business; ornamental wire hanging baskets, a wide range of wire brushes, wire fencing for use in tennis matches, and strong riddles used for sorting soil, sand and other material into different grades. This was an age of tremendous industrial growth and opportunity.

Bethel Rhodes wasted little time in taking advantage of the chance to build his business and satisfy the huge demand for the wire-based products he turned out. One particularly successful line was his range of steel wire brushes for use in foundries. These were quite an innovation at the time, and the firm was one of only two in the country to manufacture them.

International company

By the turn of the century the reputation of Bethel Rhodes Ltd. had spread not just through the locality, but to the four corners of the world. Agents in London, Paris, New York, Milan, Sydney, Melbourne and Adelaide sent orders to the expanding Keighley firm, generating valuable business and securing even more growth for the company.

Memories of Keighley

The effects of the First World War

Mr. Rhodes' retirement was short-lived, as the outbreak of the First World War caused a shortage of skilled labour. Bethel Rhodes went back to Keighley to take up the reins again, remaining there until 1923 when, at the age of 76 he returned to Morecambe.

One milestone in the history of the company, which should not go un-mentioned, was the involvement in a scheme to build a tower in Morecambe. After the Eiffel Tower was built in France there were plans to build similar structures in many coastal resorts, including, of course, Blackpool.

Most of the schemes failed, for one reason or another, including the Morecambe project. Before the termination of the scheme Bethel Rhodes had masterminded, in conjunction with a Keighley blacksmith, the construction of a huge framework for the tower.

Mr. Rhodes died at the grand old age of 85, in the seaside resort of Heysham. The year was 1932, and local papers paid glowing tributes to the man who had built up a successful business with worldwide connections, despite the many adversities bowled at him in the form of World Wars, family tragedies and recession.

Tragedy

Things didn't always go smoothly for Bethel Rhodes, and tragedy was to strike twice in 1905 and 1907 when two of his sons died at an early age. This brought the expansion of the company to a halt, with Mr. Rhodes keeping the size of the organisation to what he could control personally. By 1913 Bethel Rhodes, at the age of 66, decided to retire to his favourite resort of Morecambe, passing control over to his son Henry Rhodes.

Memories of Keighley

Fire!

In 1969 forty workers had to be evacuated when fire broke out in the works. It was the fourth Keighley fire in five days and including the Bethel Rhodes fire, the total damage was estimated at £1.5 m. The fire spread wildly, fed by a number of drums of paint stored on the floor where it began. Four fire engines were sent to the blaze, paint drums exploded and firemen were bombarded with flying slates from the roof. The blaze, amazingly enough, was brought under control within half an hour and the workers arrived the following morning to face 'mopping-up' duties which they performed in true Bethel Rhodes spirit.

Present day

Over the years Bethel Rhodes' business has grown, increasing its reputation for quality and service. The name Bethel Rhodes lives on today as a company well known for combining modern manufacturing techniques with the virtues and values of the past. The pace of life is undoubtedly faster these days, but from time to time the firm's directors spare a moment to reflect on Bethel Rhodes' achievements, and the strong foundations he laid for them to build on in Keighley.

Facing page: *Tragedy struck in 1969 when the firm's premises where engulfed by fire. Forty workers were evacuated, but, thankfully, there were no injuries.*

Left: *A 1950s view of the Bethel Rhodes works, which will, doubtless, evoke memories for many readers today.*

Memories of Keighley

Laxton Crawford, four generations of fine Mohair spinning

In 1907 George H Laxton and Gordon Holmes formed a company by the name of Holmes Laxton & Co, with George giving his technical know how and Gordon his financial expertise. They formed a partnership as worsted spinners at Vale Mills in Oakworth, travelling the country together selling their yarns. They were nick-named 'Holmes & Sutcliffe' by their competitors because they were always 'in' for so long when visiting customers.

Just prior to World War One, together with local Bradford weavers they developed new technology, spinning single mohair thread then buying in cotton thread and twisting the two together. This yarn was then sold to the weavers. Fabric made with the two elements was rather substantial but the mohair had too fine a thread to be woven by itself. Then came a process called carbonisation which dissolved the cotton, leaving the weavers with the first light-weight mohair suiting in the world.

During the 1920s Gordon Holmes founded Merrythought Toys of Ironbridge, Shropshire and in the 1930s, handed over control of it to his son, Trayton. This company is now the most famous soft toy manufacturer in the United Kingdom and is still run by the Holmes family.

The 1930s brought the depression and Holmes Laxton & Co were forced to work on a 'one week on, one week off' basis. This fair arrangement, sharing the available work went on for about three years. The yarn was exported to Germany for the manufacture of upholstery fabrics. Gradually things improved but the company was once again affected by the Second World War.

George Laxton's son (also called George) who had joined the company in the 1930s, signed up in Bingley as a volunteer in the RAF. The company found itself with a decimated workforce as the town's men clamoured to sign up. The company continued to operate however and throughout the war, women took over the work traditionally done by the men.

After the war, George Laxton was the first yarn salesman to go back to Germany to visit his old customers. Only one company remained, the rest having been destroyed by Allied bombing raids. This business sector was slow to recover as the Germans rebuilt, but in time an improvement was felt. However, by this time Holmes Laxton's machinery was becoming old and obsolete and George felt that change was needed.

Above: *Prospect Mill, Ingrow as seen in the 1920s. At the time this picture was taken the "carbonisation" process was being introduced.*

Memories of Keighley

Investing in new machinery he set up in Prospect Mill, Ingrow sharing the premises with John Haggas but maintaining the space at Vale Mill.

It was only when George Laxton (the founder) died that all business was transferred to Ingrow by Gordon Holmes and George's son. Gordon Holmes emigrated to Canada in 1966, after his retirement at the grand age of 79. Perhaps he thought he had better move as far away as possible as he had spent forty years with the company and had walked to work every day....from Ilkley! He died thirteen years later.

On Gordon's retirement John Laxton joined the company, followed by Ian Crawford. The company was changed to a partnership, releasing family funds and continued to run in this way for almost a decade. The mohair that had been supplied for upholstery was adapted to be suitable for ladies' outerwear. This was supplied to weavers in Huddersfield, Scotland and abroad.

In 1974 the company purchased a mohair twisting plant in Scotland and began producing hand knitting yarns, which were mainly mohair. The new machinery which came with the plant was too big for Ingrow so the company bought their present site at Silsden and built a new factory. Since then the company has concentrated mainly on yarns made on a 'to order' basis.

Nowadays the company sells abroad to over 80 countries and is in its fourth generation as a family business. Laxton Crawford has the most modern twisting machinery in the UK, possibly in Europe and looks forward with hope and pride to a bright future built on an exciting past.

Above: Twisting machinery being removed from Prospect Mill to be relocated at Cobbydale at Silsden.
Above, centre: Gordon Holmes in a picture from the late 1950s, together with two colleagues on a works outing to Blackpool. *Left:* Another well attended trip, again from the 1950s. *Below:* (From the left) John Pickles, Ira Sturt (storehouse man) and George Laxton. The picture dates from the late 1970s.

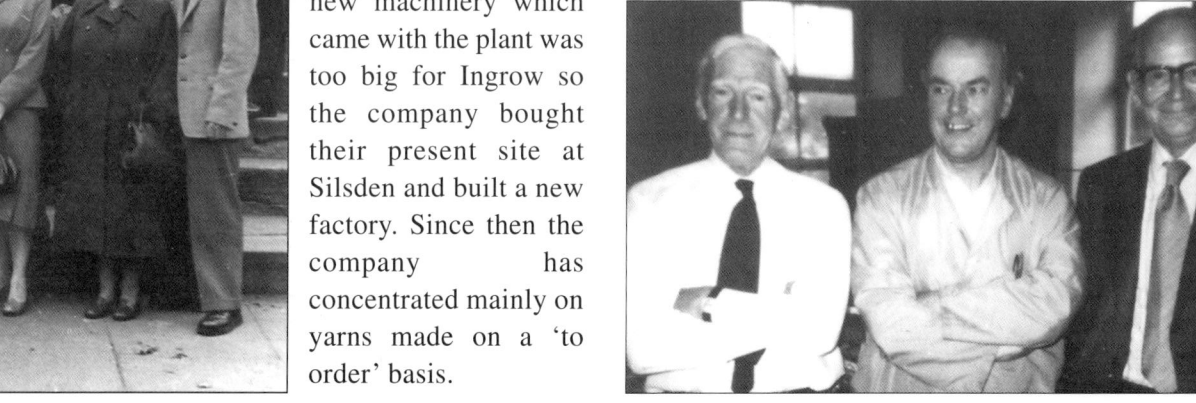

Memories of Keighley

Gesipa Blind Riveting Systems Ltd, proud to be in Keighley since 1971

Gesipa was founded in Frankfurt, West Germany, by 26 year old Dr. Hans-Georg Biermann whilst he was working on his doctorate thesis, attending the universities of Berlin, Frankfurt and Basel, where he completed his PhD. Dr. Biermann's original purpose was the acquisition and commercial exploitation, particularly through manufacture and distribution as well as licensing, of inventions and innovative manufacturing techniques in Germany and abroad. This began with a patent application for a 'hand tool for setting blind rivets by means of a compound hollow rivet with break-off mandrel'. Following this was a patent application for a 'process for the manufacture of hollow rivet fasteners with break-off mandrels' (blind rivets). The Company then resolved to develop for mass production, manufacture and sell this first German blind riveting system under the name 'GESIPA'.

In 1959 the Company's still modest product range was introduced to an international audience at the Hanover Fair. The favourable response and enthusiastic reception given to the products at this fair led to rapid further development and the Company's first international business associations. In 1965 the first Gesipa subsidiary was established as a distribution firm in Vienna, Austria. Expansion forced Gesipa to seek larger premises than those then occupied in Falkensteiner Strasse and the move was made in 1968 to its present site at Walldorf, conveniently situated for access to all major air, rail and road transport facilities and occupying a total area of 85,000 sq. m.

Following approaches made to Gesipa by a small, private company named Rivetcraft in Keighley, the company entered the UK market by purchasing the Yorkshire firm. This subsidiary was re-named 'Gesipa Fasteners Ltd.' in October of that year and continued to develop and improve upon its own range, of hand riveting tools, whilst stocking and re-selling the very successful German-produced hand and pneumatic/hydraulic riveting tool range, together with the ever-increasing range of blind rivets. Gesipa in Frankfurt continued to strive towards manufacturing improvements and new concepts, at the same time stepping up its public relations efforts to equate the name Gesipa with quality and craftsmanship.

Several leading automobile manufacturers were already clients of Gesipa and as a high-visibility advertising vehicle, Dr. Biermann chose racing cars. To this end, Gesipa acquired two Porsche racing cars which entered the European racing circuits and gained high placings

Gesipa's new premises at Dalton Lane, Worth Village were opened by the late Councillor Bob Cryer (second left from the sign) in March 1979

Memories of Keighley

on several occasions, including winning the 1971 Interserie Championship. By the mid 1970s Gesipa was ready to enter the American market and began with the setting up of Gesipa Fasteners Inc. U.S.A. in Trenton, New Jersey in 1975. It was a production plant of 7,500 sq. m. giving adequate production, stores and administration facilities to supply the greatest single market in the world with an extensive range of imperial-sized blind rivets, rivet nuts and tools to suit. In the meantime, further sales and holding Companies had been founded in Canada, Switzerland and Ecuador.

Blind riveting is a technology in worldwide use today as no other fastening system joins so many different types of materials, hard or soft, so fast and reliably. Industry was first to see its many advantages and this system is now used in everything from jet aircraft production to simple household articles.

Much of Gesipa's success is based on its constant aim for top quality, beginning with the selection of raw materials which are subjected to constant checks to ensure they conform exactly to their demands. A total of more than 800 types of rivets are now available from Gesipa in both dome and countersunk heads in all types of materials. The end product is again subject to a series of stringent trials using the very latest testing techniques. Exactly the same careful tests are carried out with the riveting tool production; six types of hand tools, two pneumatic/mechanical, three pneumatic/hydraulic and the very latest fully-automatic machine for mass production.

Backed by the knowledge and strength of the parent-Company and its products, in 1971/2 Gesipa Fasteners in Keighley began to expand its stocks of rivets and German-produced tools, whilst at the same time up-dating and improving its own small range of hand tools. The slow process of entering into the U.K. rivet market began, using the major advantages of high-quality products of proven reliability, prompt delivery and customer service. The Keighley concern strove to train and retain a nucleus of conscientious and loyal personnel, the basis of any forward-looking company that realises investment cannot be made only in capital goods.

Gesipa's modern day premises at Dalton Lane

By 1976, it was apparent Keighley was beginning to resemble a 'sardine tin' and steps were taken to find the ideal site for a purpose-built office and factory block to allow for the very necessary expansion. This site was roughly 200 yards from the doorstep of their then leased premises, in an area known as Worth Village, giving the company a total area of 15,000 sq. m.

It seemed unlikely at that time that the company would ever fill it, but fill it they did. Just three years later, they invested in their first rivet-making machinery and demand was such that in 1989, the company had to add a further 15,000 sq. m. to the building to house all the machinery, raw materials etc.

Today, the company has 34 machines involved in the production of rivets, but Gesipa believes that the most important asset of any company is its people. Machinery will not run without people, and how well the machine runs depends on those people. It is this philosophy that has led Gesipa to the enormous success story it is today.

Gesipa's workforce in the 1970s, before the move to Dalton Lane took place.

Memories of Keighley

Landis Lund - engineering excellence for over a century-and-a-half

The history of engineering over the last two hundred years is illustrated by the factories that have functioned on the company site during that time. General engineers, serving the burgeoning textile industry in Yorkshire and Lancashire, followed millwrights who followed wheelwrights who had ousted iron founders.

The first of these, John Clapham, began his business as Queen Victoria began her reign. Two years later he sold it and went to Canada with his brother, Thomas. The pair returned after a short stay, bought the business back and took a third brother, William, into partnership. Things moved slowly at first, but by 1850 they had built the Wellington Foundry and in 1870 another was set up in Lawkholme Lane.

Clapham Brothers continued after the demise of John, Thomas and William, flourishing under many directors but keeping the name until 1932.

One of the many grinding machines manufactured by John Lund Limited.

During the war years John Lund Limited, like many other businesses at that time, was requisitioned for war work. Women played a big part, taking the place of husbands, sons and brothers while they served in the forces.

Having evolved a fine range of high class grinding machines, meeting the demand for Precise work and maximum production. John Lund coined the name PRECIMAX for the company's grinding machines and fine borers and won glory for the firm by exhibiting them in the Olympia Machine Tool Exhibition. In 1958, after being acquired by Landis Tool Company of Pennsylvania of USA, the company became Landis-Lund Ltd. and produced crankshaft and camshaft grinding machines, the range of Landis machines being introduced gradually as the work force was trained to manufacture each model. Ten years later, Litton, of Beverley Hills, California,

Memories of Keighley

important to the management, people. The company now aims to maintain its position as a European market leader for cam and crankshaft grinding machines and to expand into the transmission industry. It plans to place greater emphasis on the development of Eastern European markets and to further expand existing markets in Australia, India, the Pacific rim and South Africa.

In its bid to continue to lead the market, Landis Lund gives high priority to the training of local young people. Apprenticeship programmes and graduate training schemes are constantly in progress and the company sees it as a privilege to utilise and promote local talent.

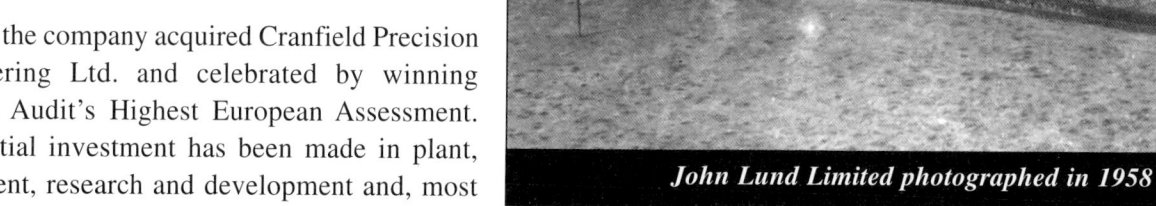

John Lund Limited photographed in 1958

A 1950s photograph showing the John Lund workshop

acquired the company but allowed it to keep its name. It won two Queen's awards, for Industry in 1970 and for Export Achievement in 1982.

In 1985, when Landis Lund became a Division of Litton UK Ltd., eighty percent of its output was being exported to the world's automotive manufacturers. Prestigious awards continued to be bestowed on the company. In 1987, there was another Queen's award, this time for technological achievement. 1990 brought the Renault Audit Joint Highest Award for European Assessment, and 1991 an award for high achievement in customer care, the BS 5750/120 9001 Re-certification in 1994. In 1994 Litton Industries consolidated its commercial businesses into the newly formed separate company - Western Atlas.

In 1995 the company acquired Cranfield Precision Engineering Ltd. and celebrated by winning Renault Audit's Highest European Assessment. Substantial investment has been made in plant, equipment, research and development and, most

Memories of Keighley

The Hattersley story - from Luddites to hi-tech narrow fabrics

Around 1784, Richard Hattersley moved from his home in Ecclesfield, Sheffield to Leeds where he served his apprenticeship at Kirkstall Forge. In 1789 he decided to set up his own business at Stubbings Mill at Aireworth, manufacturing screws, nuts and bolts. The mill soon gained the nickname 'Screw Mill'. His business thrived and he expanded the range of products to include spindles, rollers and other spares for the textile trade. By 1800 it was necessary for him to move to more spacious premises in South Street, Keighley.

Richard Hattersley, founder of the company

Hattersley versus the Luddites

Richard's son, George came into the business and eventually took over its running. In 1834 he was asked to build a powered loom for weaving worsted cloth. Power looms had been used for some time for weaving cotton but it was generally agreed that good worsted cloth could only be produced on hand looms. George Hattersley proved them wrong. Later that year he produced the first worsted power loom, which was promptly broken up on its way to a customer in Bradford by the Luddites, a band of hand loom weavers, frightened for their livelihoods. Eventually, George was successful in convincing the hand loom weavers to change their minds by offering them jobs in his factory and the company went on unhindered, with a bulging order book.

The 'Dobby'

By 1867, George Hattersley & Sons, as the company was renamed, invented and patented the first 'heald' lifting machine, which later became known as 'the dobby'. This was a major breakthrough for the textile industry as it allowed infinitely more intricate patterns to be woven, making power looms far more versatile than ever before. Hattersley's became more prosperous as the years went by, peaking at 1,100 employees just prior to the First World War by which time they were producing a vast range of weaving, warping and winding machinery for all known applications world wide.

Cabbage Mills

In 1908 their first smallware (narrow fabric) loom was built but was rejected at the outset by the trade, despite the firm's reputation, on the grounds that it wouldn't be a commercial success. Undeterred by this temporary setback, the company

A Geo Hattersley 'Scammel' delivery truck driven by Billy Gill - circa 1947. He is transporting a consignment of Hattersley 4 by 1 drop box looms.

bought Cabbage Mills at Greengate, Keighley and filled it with their own machines and started producing tapes and webbings. This proved an unqualified success and with the advent of the war, the company worked around the clock, producing tapes for the services and making their smallware looms for the trade in general. New premises were bought at Greengate at the onset of the war and narrow fabric weaving has remained there ever since.

The Hattersley Standard Loom

In 1921 the company designed and built what was to become known as the Hattersley Standard Loom, a machine which sold by the thousands worldwide, leading to great financial success for the company, right up to the 1960s. In an effort to keep buoyant in the 1970s, when textile mills were being closed

A Hattersley heavy wire loom which was patented in 1913. Standing beside it is Mr Smith Midgeley who was the assembly line foreman at the time the picture was taken circa 1930.

Memories of Keighley

been with the company since its independence in 1971. "Tony" continues to drive the company forward with the same determination, enthusiasm and foresight of his predecessors.

With an eye to the future, the company is expanding the webbing trade into Europe and the breadth of Hattersley's customer base takes in such diverse products as equestrian items, oil filter removal tools, husky dog harnesses and hot air balloons!

The Company's Target

Good old fashioned service coupled with top quality goods, at extremely competitive prices, hold the secret to success in the modern day world of international business. Hattersley's (Narrow Fabrics) Ltd recognises that this philosophy is the only way to achieve continued progress. The complete package offered by the company shows there is no reason why the Hattersley name shouldn't go from strength to strength for the next hundred years, and hopefully beyond.

The Queen's coronation in 1953 was celebrated at Hattersley's Greengate mill in great style.

A Hattersley exhibition stand in Roubaix, France in 1911. This exhibition was the only 'Grand Prix' for weaving machinery and Hattersleys received the highest awards.

all over the country, the company diversified into high quality garden furniture production and sub contract engineering work. It wasn't enough. A gradual decline continued until in 1984, the directors decided that George Hattersley should cease trading. Fortunately, the narrow fabric section of the business had already become a separate division in 1971 and taken the name of Hattersley (Narrow Fabrics) Ltd, albeit controlled by the same directors and shareholders as George Hattersley.

The New Company

This company, headed by Mr A C (Robin) Smith, became established as one of the world's largest manufacturers of wicks for paraffin appliances and as one of the country's leading producers of narrow fabrics to the fashion trade and industry in general.

In 1987 Robin Smith was forced to retire through ill health and passed on his position to Anthony Woodyatt, the current managing director, who has

Memories of Keighley

Keighley College - bringing further education to the area for over 170 years

Keighley College, as it is now known, was founded in 1825 as 'The Society for Mutual Instruction in Mechanics, Experimental Philosophy and Mathematics' and before long became known as Keighley Mechanics Institute. Doctor George Birkbeck, a Yorkshireman and the son of a Quaker banker was a professor at what was to become the Glasgow Royal Technical College. Dr Birkbeck recognised the need for a facility for all members of the community. He believed poor circumstance and background should be no bar to the acquisition of knowledge.

The educational elite had little time for this view but undeterred by this he persisted and 75 attended his first classes which soon rose to over 500. From this beginning grew the movement which brought education to the masses as well as laying the foundations for the technical colleges, public libraries and universities which are an integral part of British life.

In Keighley, the adult and further education movement was championed by Swire Smith (later knighted) whose part in the early development of the college is recognised by the Sir Swire Smith Hall, although the key figures in its formative years were four local tradesmen; John Farish (a feed maker),

Above: A modern picture of Keighley College.
Right: An August 1967 photograph of the extension to what was then called Keighley Technical College.

Work started on constructing the College's present main building at the junction of Cavendish Street and North Street in March 1967, five years to the month after fire destroyed the Mechanics Institute which housed the College's Art School, Textile Department and the Municipal Hall. The work was completed and students started classes in new, spacious surroundings in September 1968.

Memories of Keighley

John Bradley (a painter), William Dixon (a tailor) and John Haigh (a joiner). Along with a secretary (John Bradley) they formed the initial committee and called the first meeting on 24th January 1825 at the house of John Farish.

The institute grew and continued to provide adult education and skill training to meet the needs of the newly industrialised Keighley. Land was leased in 1833 on North Street for £2 per annum which when built upon, provided the college's first home, remaining there until it was demolished in 1968 as part of the town centre redevelopment scheme. However the college had moved from this building long before this time, moving to its present location at the junction between Cavendish Street and North Street.

The Mechanics Institute not only provided the adult education in the district but also provided support for elementary education as covered by the 1870 Act introduced by the Bradford MP WE Forster. It was Swire Smith and his friends who, drawing on their experience of continental education, realised that the establishment of a school board was essential to provide the elementary education for the young of the area on whom the continued success of the Institute's broadening education aspirations depended. At the turn of the century a clock tower was built to the memory of Prince Smith, the father of Swire Smith. This landmark stood until 1962 when it was gutted in a blaze. It was around the turn of the century when, with the establishment of the Technical Instruction Act, the Institute became known as Keighley Technical College. It was at that time that the college had its first telephone line installed. It seems a huge step to consider that nowadays the pupils at Keighley College use the telephone to connect to the world via the internet!

In April 1993 the college was incorporated, leaving the control of Bradford Metropolitan District Council, acting autonomously. Everyone benefited from this move which has placed the college in a strong position for future growth.

The college has acquired another site in Chesham Street and a £multi-million ongoing investment programme is allowing the college to fulfil its plans to centralise and improve its provisions at the refurbished Harold Town Building (Chesham Street) and the Cavendish Street site.

Above left: This view along North Street in the 1930s demonstrates the focal point that the clock-tower of the Mechanics' Institute provided. It stood until 1962 when it was destroyed by a spectacular fire. Left: This plaque commemorates the building of the Mechanics' Institute clock-tower in 1892.

Keighley College and True North Books thank Charles B Curtis for his extensive research from which the College's story was drawn. The full text of his dissertation, 'The Origins and Early History of Keighley Technical College' is available in the College Library.

Around the town centre

Left: A view of a section of High Street which was captured on camera in the early months of 1967. A variety of popular shops can be seen on the picture, including Lord and Co., responsible for furnishing the homes of countless Keighley families, Wilson's Nurseryland, the company which provided the prams and later push-chairs for most of the area's babies, and Appleyard's the bakers in mock-tudor shop which sported the familiar 'Turog' sign for more years than we care to remember. Smith's the tobacconists' completes the roll call, their double-fronted shop serving the smoking population of Keighley for decades. The new shopping areas in Keighley would attract the 'national multiples' - professional retail organisations who sought an outlet in every significant town.

Right: A 1963 view of The Cross and the junction of High Street and Low Street featuring the number 27 bus service to Haworth and Marsh. The picture affords a rare view of the ladies' public lavatory situated on the corner of Bridge Street and High Street which, uniquely, incorporated a hat shop for many years. 1963 was easily the most dramatic year of the decade; major events occurred on the national and international stage, including the assassination of President John F.Kennedy, followed days later by the killing of the man accused of his murder; the Profumo affair rocked British politics, resulting in the resignation of John Profumo, the Cabinet Minister after admitting that he misled Parliament about his relationship with Christine Keeler. The 'Great Train Robbery' saw daring thieves steal over £1 million from a Post Office mobile railway carriage on the Glasgow to London mail train. On a brighter note, Winston Churchill was made an honourary citizen of the United States of America.

Memories of Keighley

The King's Arms public house features strongly in this picture from 1966. There seems to be little out of the ordinary in this view of a 'typical' town-centre pub on the corner of a busy street, but there is an interesting background to the establishment which belies its very anonymous appearance. The King's Arms has a very long history, and was once an old coaching inn complete with stables and barns. More recently it was the headquarters of Keighley Rugby League Football Club in the early years of the club's development. Players would change their clothes at the King's Arms before departing for the match. The match referee would change there also, before taking a cab to the ground. Sadly the King's Arms' place in history was not enough to save it from the demolition men, and it was pulled down shortly after this picture was taken.

Memories of Keighley

Left: A busy shopping scene showing Low Street as it was in October 1967. many familiar names can be seen on the 'modern' shop fronts which have been added to the turn-of-the-century buildings which graced the popular shopping area for several decades. Freeman Hardy and Willis, the famous shoe retailer supplied the footwear for the people of Keighley (and much of the rest of the Country) for generations. Other well-known national chains had premises on Low Street, including John Collier (didn't we all buy our wedding suits there?), Timothy Whites the chemists and, most famous of all, Marks and Spencer. Throughout the country at this time the national retail chains were demanding better access for deliveries and bright modern retail units capable of attracting the modern shopper.

Right: Guaranteed to bring back memories of shopping in Low Street, this photograph was taken towards the end of 1962. The branch office of the Yorkshire Evening News enjoyed this prominent position in Keighley and the windows shown here are full of posters promoting their sports coverage. The company was later swallowed up by a competitor as radio and television news services began their gradual but irreversible attack on the circulation of regional newspapers. The Austin A60 van belonging to Raymond Simpson and Son, a painting contractor based in Riddleston would have been a familiar sight around the roads of Keighley. Freeman Hardy Willis was a dominant force in the retail footwear industry, not just in Keighley of course, but throughout the whole of Britain. Their shop along Low Street was as popular as any, situated as it was alongside Liptons.

Memories of Keighley

Right: The Hare and Hounds public house was a popular town centre watering hole for people who enjoyed their pint and a natter with the regulars. It stood on the corner of Low Street and Wellington Street. This picture dates from 1960. It was a time at the very dawn of the reconstruction work which was to change Keighley forever. Some younger readers may be surprised to see Curry's electrical store next to the Hare and Hounds. A wide range or radios and domestic appliances were sold by them in Keighley, even as far back as 1960. There were several other popular and well-patronised businesses along the street, including the Singer sewing machine shop and Wild's the confectioners. By the mid-1960s the properties featured here were pulled down in order to make way for the Worth Way and the Social Security offices.

Left: A small part of the extensive Co-op and Keighley Industrial Society premises on Brunswick Street and Low Street. The organisation's offices were located in the block on Brunswick Street. The two adjacent windows here give an impression of the width of the range of products available from the organisation, from the latest fashions in mens' shirts to Outspan oranges and other fresh fruit from around the world just a few yards away. This picture was taken on a crisp November day. Note the two ladies in the photograph and the sense of purpose in their stride off on their shopping expedition. Where are they now, we wonder?

Memories of Keighley

Proudly proclaiming the fact that it was established in 1860, the Co-operative store on the corner of Brunswick Street and Low Street dominates this photograph. The picture dates from the summer of 1961 and the summer sale is in full swing at 'Maxwells' on the right of the picture. Note the uneven surface of the road and footpath in the picture and the sense of congestion and disorganisation evoked by the scene. Most of this was to change in the impending redevelopment, and a generally-welcomed sense of order would descend upon Keighley over the next decade. 1961 saw the abolition of Farthings and the commencement of negotiations which were to take Britain into the European Common Market, and the world of films was rocked by the death of Gary Cooper at the age of 60.

Memories of Keighley

The new Co-Op was opened to the shoppers of Keighley in April 1966. It is seen here under construction in July 1966, the same year that a new bridge across Hanover Street was opened as part of the central development scheme. The Co-Op was a major element in the upgrading of Keighley's town centre. The retail organisation was, as it is now, a symbol of reputable, long established family shopping, and the decision to invest in a state-of-the-art modern store in Keighley was a welcome vote of thanks. Less welcome was the seemingly endless construction work in the town, not just relating to the building of the Co-Op, but with all the road widening and associated work which was necessary to bring her retail environment up to the standards of neighbouring towns and cities such as Bradford and Leeds. Piledrivers, concrete mixers, builders and trucks would try the patience of Keighley's townsfolk for many years. Most would simply shrug and put it down as the price of progress.

Memories of Keighley

Right: April 1966. A hive of activity beneath the the photographer in this elevated view of Cook Lane. The scene here speaks for itself, a handful of shoppers going about their business, blissfully unaware that the photographer is recording events for generations to come. Cook Lane is famous as the place where Timothy Taylor started his famous brewing business almost a century and a half ago in 1858. Keighley's brewing pioneer had formerly been in the tailoring trade with a shop in Low Street, but acquired the skills of a maltster and brewer before starting his own brewery and making his fortune in the licensed trade. In the early days of his business empire Taylor had two public houses in Keighley, the first being The Volunteer's Arms in Lawkholme Lane and the second the New Inn at Bocking. By 1863 Taylor's brewing activities relocated to Knowle Spring, a move made necessary by constantly increasing demand for his beer.

Left: Ramsbottoms was a well-known name in the field of television rental and record sales in Keighley. Their business on Cook Lane is featured in this photograph from 1967. Further along the street Rhodes and Padget's shop lies under the shadow of the soon-to-be-completed retail development. There were many changes going on in Keighley at this time, indeed there were many national and international events which would have been of interest too. Harold Wilson was trying to convince the country that his tight economic policy including the devalued Pound would soon see Britain booming; seventeen 'pirate' disc jockeys who had been working for various radio stations were given £30-per-week jobs at the BBC, mostly in connection to the forthcoming Radio One service; Donald Campbell (45) died during his bid to break the land speed record on Coniston Water after achieving a speed of 276 mph. His body was never found.

Memories of Keighley

Left: Men at work - a familiar sight in the centre of Keighley during the redevelopment of the town. Note the Woolworth sign in the centre of the photograph. The world-famous retailer had been associated with Keighley since 1927 and opened their reconstructed premises in the town in 1958. This picture was taken in July 1968 and, by this time, the development was very well advanced. Two months earlier a commemorative stone had been laid by the Mayor, Cllr. A. Greenwood to mark the progress that had been made so far. The plan was to complete all the improvements by the end of 1969.

Much controversy followed the decision to erect a massive bronze statue and modern mural with money donated by the developers in the heart of the new shopping centre. The issue attracted coverage on local television and in the local and regional press.

Right: The offices of the North Eastern Gas Board and the Direct Walk Around Store dominate this view of Cook Lane. Both properties were pulled down less than four years after this picture was taken. It may just be possible to make out the array of bright new cookers in the Gas Showrooms which would have been a tempting sight to the housewives of Keighley as they passed through this busy thoroughfare. The Direct Walk Round Store offered many attractive cut-price lines and the notices in the window describe it as a 'furniture supermarket'. Both establishments would have been well supported by the countless thousands of families who moved out of the sub-standard housing close to the town centre and into the flats and Corporation houses further afield. The 'sixties' marked the time when 'consumerism' began to take off in Britain and this was part of the reason for the urgency felt by Keighley's planners to reconstruct the town's retail facilities and keep up with the increasing demands of national retailers.

Memories of Keighley

In the present day, pub landlords seem to come and go almost as often as their customers. This was not always the case, a fact illustrated by the last lady to have her name above the door of the Queen Street Arms, better known as the *Grinning Rat* by regulars at the pub. Mrs Edith Riley, was a spritely 73-year-old who's father had been the licensee as far back as 1903. This picture was taken in 1961, just five years before most of the buildings seen in this picture were cleared to make way for the new retail shopping centre.

The variety of late 1950s and very early 1960s motor vehicles adds to the nostalgic character of this photograph. The dark triangle at the bottom right of the picture is the front of a motorcycle combination (motorbike and sidecar to the uninitiated,) a very popular method of transport among 'bikers' who found themselves with a growing family.

Memories of Keighley

Left: Variously described as an 'eyesore' and a 'blot on the landscape', the piece of land which became the site for the Town Hall Square was once a builders' yard. The original reason for creating the square was to provide an open space for people wishing to hold public meetings in Keighley. At the time, around the turn of the century, Temperance meetings attracting upwards of a thousand people were held at Townfield Gate, later to become the location of the bus station. This caused congestion in the central area of town and great inconvenience to traders and pedestrians alike. The War Memorial was erected in 1924 and unveiled in December of the same year in front of an appreciative gathering of no less than 25,000 people - over half of the town's population. In excess of £6,000 had been raised by public subscription to pay for the bronze statue 'Peace Victory' which features a wreath in one hand and a branch in the other, and standing 35 feet above the neatly laid out square below. During the Great War over 900 Keighley men gave their lives, so it is unsurprising that the unveiling received such support.

Right: Situated at the top of Cavendish Street, opposite Keighley Library, The Mechanic's Institute was a prestigious building and a great source of pride to local people. It housed the Municipal Hall, The Keighley Trade and Grammar School and Keighley's School of Art. The clock tower on the building was the much-photographed focal point of the town centre for many years.

The large saloon car in the photograph is a Humber, a luxurious, six cylinder executive vehicle capable of cruising at 90mph in a cocoon of leather, walnut and deep pile carpets. It would have been the type of car used by successful businessmen and those at the top of their profession. Sadly, few survive today.

Memories of Keighley

Left: A view looking down Lawkholme Crescent dating from October 1962. The Cavendish Hotel is visible at the end of the street, and the characterful 1960s vehicles parked on the roadside add atmosphere and evoke feelings of nostalgia in the scene. This was the age of successful black and white British films and the scene featured here could be taken from any one of them.

Below: A view of Cavendish Street dating from 1962 in a picture dominated by the premises of Ryley & Sons (stationers) Ltd. The buildings on the right of the picture were scheduled for demolition. Up until the 1960s Cavendish Street was Keighley's premier shopping area. The street itself was wide and airy and it is best known for the overhead canopy which provided sheltered window-shopping along a lengthy section of the block. The covered walkway dates back to 1878, though it was extensively renovated in 1950.

Right: This photograph was taken from the old Gas Board offices and shows a shopping scene on Cooke Lane. Some of the earliest redevelopment work had been carried out in this area of Keighley, all of which was designed to separate motor vehicles and their unpleasant fumes from pedestrian traffic.

Wide, modern walkways would replace the narrow congested streets, and multi-storey car parking would ensure that shoppers would be able to park their vehicles just a short way away from the new shops. The shops themselves would be serviced via discreet efficient loading areas, often on a different level to the pedestrian area, so that the centre of town would no longer be clogged up with delivery vans. Shrubs and flower beds would add to the illusion of cleanliness and spaciousness in order to prepare Keighley for the start of the 'consumer age'.

Memories of Keighley

Right: A wet January in 1965 is shown here in this photograph of Station Bridge. The damp cobbles and poorly maintained road surface create a gloomy atmosphere, and the style of the clinical modern street lamps clashes with the appearance of the traditional century-old shops which line the street. A month after this scene was captured the shops and offices shown here, along with adjoining properties in Low Mill Lane were offered for sale in a public auction.

There were several things to celebrate in the Britain of 1965; the opening of the Telecom Tower in London and Jim Clark winning the World Racing Car Championship.

Left: An elevated view along Cavendish Street which dates from 1971. The scene will still appear to be modern to most people despite the fact that it is over a quarter of a century old. The foreground is dominated by the the Technical College and the rather box-like ornamental flower beds beneath it. The Technical College was built upon the site of the former Mechanic's Institute and Cavendish Street Chapel. The modern, plain street lamps lining Cavendish Street stand like soldiers on sentry duty, and the Town Hall Square's flower beds are just in view on the right of the picture.

Wheels of time

Left: Happy faces in this delightful scene from 1932, marking the end of the 'trackless' era in Keighley. The earliest *Trackless* transport services had been introduced in 1913 as a result of the poor condition of the area's tramlines and rolling stock. The vehicles were never very successful for a variety of technical reasons. At the time this picture was taken they were about to be superseded by motor buses which had been running alongside them since 1924. Keighley was the first town to abandon traditional trams and was unusual in as much as it offered services covering relatively long distances away from the town centre. Neighbouring towns such as Colne and Hebden Bridge were linked from the very earliest years of Keighley's public transport services. The former Mayor and M.P for Keighley, Sir Robert Clough, speaking in 1932, cited the excellence of Keighley's transport system for the slow development of her town centre, both in terms of population growth and 'rateable value'.

Memories of Keighley

Right: The bus station as it was in 1962, featuring the transport offices which had been built there in 1940. The rather plain, utilitarian design is generally pleasing to the eye despite the clumsy looking pillars holding up the surrounding canopy. At one time the building housed a waiting room and various facilities for staff, including changing rooms. Construction of the facility and the general facelift of the bus station as a whole was considered to be long overdue by most of the public transport-using residents of Keighley.

Facing page, small picture: An imposing view of a Keighley Corporation Tramways car which dates from 1922. Electric trams had been a familiar sight on the streets of Keighley - and beyond, since they were introduced in 1904. Indeed, on the first day of their operation over 3,500 local people took a ride on the new vehicles, such was the interest in the new mode of transport. This covered tramcar would have looked impressive in its glossy crimson and cream hand-painted livery, but by the time this scene was recorded the future of Keighley's trams was already in doubt. Two years later the frequently documented trackless era began and Keighley acquired the distinction of being the first town in the country to completely do away with traditional trams.

Left: The cafe and snack bar overlooking the bus station was a popular refuge for people hoping to escape the wind and rain in the bleaker weather which afflicted the area at times. Keen eyes may just be able to make out the sign on the bay at the left of the picture 'No. 9, Spring Bank', and some may recall waiting there for their service from time to time. Note too the tall electric light featured here. Some readers may remember how the top would sway and rattle in the swirling currents which characterised the area. This photograph was taken in 1963, a time when the curvaceous Austin A30 outside the snack bar was starting to appear rather outdated alongside the modern Minis which were taking the motoring public by storm. One of my fondest memories is of trips to Blackpool as a child with mother, father, aunt and uncle, crammed into a trusty dark green Austin A35, fish and chips on the sea front and not arriving back home until the early hours of the morning. Happy days indeed.

Memories of Keighley

An interesting view of the bus station site as it was during reconstruction. The date was 1970 and the new facility was being built on the same site as the existing station. The work involved the creation of new bus stands on the perimeter of the station, along with office blocks and toilets formed in a style to blend in with the surrounding shops. The passenger shelters were lit by fluorescent lights and offered more cover than the ones they replaced. Many people considered the station to be long overdue and the growth in passenger transport certainly made the improvements essential. One major benefit to the town as a whole was the removal of many, if not most of the bus stops around the town centre.

This was to reduce congestion on the roads in the centre as fewer buses would be picking up passengers there and holding up the traffic. The old bus station handled 132,000 departures in the year before it was improved. The following year saw this figure increase by more 100,000.

Memories of Keighley

After six years hard work, battles with a plethora of red tape and legal complications, fundraising and battles in the face of public scepticism, the Worth Valley line was ready for the crucial Ministry of Transport inspection. It was May 1968 and the inspector was Col. J R H Robertson OBE. Everyone was thrilled to hear that the line and rolling stock was given a clean bill of health and the path was clear to organise the opening ceremony which was to be conducted by the Mayor of Keighley Alderman J H Waterworth. At the official opening two engines were used, an Ivatt Class 2 Locomotive No. 41241 and a U.S Tank Locomotive No. 30072 along with 6 carriages. At 2.35pm the train, carrying the official opening party and festooned with flags and bunting, chugged out of Keighley station to great cheering and more than a few tearful eyes. For many of the people who attended the opening it was simply a great day. To members of the Society it was the achievement of a lifetime's dream.

Memories of Keighley

From a small workshop to the country's best selling Ford agency - 80 years of motoring heritage

The well known Keighley Ford dealership was established as a motor engineering company in 1918 by Walter Burgess. The business was also an agency for Arrol Johnson cars (a little known make which was produced in Scotland) and began in a small workshop in Hanover Street, Keighley. The company was incorporated on August 25, 1923 and was appointed one of the earliest Ford dealerships in October of that year. Walter Burgess died shortly afterwards and the company's auditor, Edward Clough, along with Mrs Burgess formed a Limited Company.

War years

In 1930 Jonathan Wilby bought shares in the company and brought in Richard Etherington in November. This team helped the small company to grow, so much so in fact that just four years later it was awarded the Ford Main Dealership for 1934 - 1935.

Due to trade restrictions during the Second World War, the company had to invest its own surplus capital (to the sum of £500) to keep itself afloat. The Company made very little profit throughout these difficult times. Richard Etherington was appointed Managing Director in 1942 and the following year the directors decided to look for land in order to build a new garage.

An early Ford open-topped Model 'T', dating from the 1920s. Walter Burgess began his business selling cars such as this.

The Walter Burgess premises in Hanover Street, taken in 1931. The firm still occupies the same site to this day, but has grown in size considerably

over for storage purposes in 1949 and in the 1950s and 1960s the company diversified to specialise in commercial vehicle requirements such as refuse wagons, ambulances and ice cream vans, supplied to Fred's Ices - a well known ice cream retailer at the time. These were made on site and fitted with Ford chassis and engines.

In 1953 the Hanover street premises were purchased and The tractor and service department at Steeton was taken

Memories of Keighley

three years later, after hard work and commitment the new workshop was officially opened. A quirk of fate helped the company to expand in the late 1960s. The plans for the new Keighley town centre showed that a new multi-storey car park was to be erected directly across from the Hanover Street workshop. It was a dream come true with all those prospective buyers just yards away. Richard Etherington approached Ford with his ideas for a new and bright showroom and they readily agreed. The new showroom was built within two years, before the car park was erected. In 1971 the tenancy at Steeton was terminated and the storage facilities were transferred to Dalton Lane. The following year a meeting between Richard Etherington and the fleet sales manager of the Ford Motor Company saw 850 brand new cars delivered to Burgess before the end of September to supply to the Clock Car Centre, which was a national company based in Keighley.

In 1972 and 1973 500 new Escorts and Cortinas a month were being delivered until the hire purchase laws were changed.

Generations

The company has a strong client base which has built up over the years. Generations of the same families return to Burgess Ford for their cars. This is helped by the Company's policy of 'putting themselves in their customers shoes'. In other words Burgess Ford insists on making buying a pleasant experience. With the combined experience of years in the trade, the company is one of the few independent Main Dealerships in the north of England. Its Dalton Lane premises house its busy Service, Parts and Bodyshop departments.

The company was awarded ISO 9002 for quality, for all of its departments in December 1992, the first Ford dealer in the North to be awarded this certificate. Ever conscious of the need to expand, the company is presently in the process of looking for new premises or expanding the old, to afford more display area for its ever popular cars and vans.

The Hanover Street premises in 1949. The van outside the showroom, emblazoned with the Burgess name would take parts to local customers

Memories of Keighley

This picture dates from June 1965 and features dozens of people at a promotional day for the Keighley and Worth Valley Railway Preservation Society which had been formed just two years earlier. In the years after the society took on the task of reopening the line a tremendous amount of renovation and restoration work was done by the army of unpaid volunteers.

Everything was geared towards a rigorous Ministry of Transport inspection of the facilities, engines, track and operating procedures which was required before the line could be opened to the public. Membership of the society reflected the obstacles being faced by the society at the time. It quickly became clear that there was far more to the project than an ability to drive steam engines up and down the line! Thankfully, for everyone in Keighley and the surrounding area, as well as the countless number of rail enthusiasts in the world, they saw the job through to the end.

At the shops

Right: An unusual, early 1960s, view of Low Street from the Gott and Butterfield Arcade. Three pairs of eyes can be seen studying various items of camping and gardening equipment through the plate glass, the little boy in the picture no doubt pestering his dad to buy the latest tent or primus stove!

Below: It was 'Overall Fortnight' at the Famous Army Stores outlet in October 1962. Next door Melia's Provisions did a roaring trade and if 'Sir' needed a haircut, the skilled hands of J R Doggett were a few feet further along the street. D.E.R was one place to get your rented telly and Crockatts the same day cleaners had a busy shop next door to that. The most imposing building on the street, in fact this part of Keighley, was the Midland Bank. In 1965 a section of North Street was demolished to make way for the construction of a new Midland Bank to replace the one featured here. The solitary building on the extreme right of the picture was occupied by Keighley Printers when this photograph was taken.

Memories of Keighley

Warm September sunshine bathed these shoppers on Low Street in 1961. Familiar business names include Barwick and Haggas the watchmakers and jewellers, Curry's the popular electrical appliance retailer, and the Outsize shop which supplied ladies fashions for the fuller figure. The trusty Austin A35 van seen here gives an impression of the era and will bring back fond memories of the lovely little vehicles to the hundreds of readers who, like me, once owned one. Parking restrictions were to blight the lives of local traders in Keighley from about this time onwards. The effect of yellow lines was to disrupt the patterns of customer buying habits built up over any years. Shops which relied upon small, regular purchases, such as newsagents, were often most badly affected, and the phenomenon was widely reported in the local press as small businesses suffered.

Memories of Keighley

A busy shopping scene in Low Street, recorded in September 1961. No wonder it was busy, for at this time Low Street was one of the main shopping areas in Keighley, as evidenced by the presence of the Marks and Spencer store on the right of the picture. This branch of Britain's best loved retailer was opened initially in 1912, but it was extensively modernised and reopened in the form seen here in March 1935. Further extensions took place in July 1969.

The influence of a Marks and Spencer store on any town cannot be under-estimated; many retail specialists consider the location of 'M & S' to be the very centre of shopping activity in a town, and prospective tennants or owners of retail property routinely assess the value of their new premises in relation to its proximity to Mark and Spencer. Their power to attract customers has been finely tuned over decades.

Memories of Keighley

A thought-provoking scene showing Cooke Lane and the 'Direct Walk Round Store'. The power of advertising was graphically demonstrated in July 1969 when notices proclaiming this closing down sale appeared in the local press and caused a queue of bargain hunters nearly 200 yards long. Further along the street the North Eastern Gas Board was also having a sale, though it seemed rather less popular than the one being held at the shop next door! The closure of these two businesses was caused by the impending town centre redevelopment, and the properties featured here would soon be swept away to make room for bigger and better facilities constructed by the Murrayfield Real Estate Company.

Memories of Keighley

Right: Construction underway at the Worth Way branch of Morrisons supermarket in this picture dating from July 1968. This was the first Morrisons store outside the Bradford boundary and, at the time, Keighley's largest retail shop. Floor space was 58,000 sq. ft. and shoppers were assured of quick service with the 18 modern checkouts in place. The store was staffed by over 100 employees and it boasted a coffee bar, wide aisles and ample parking for customers. The store was completed on time for its opening on October 9 1968, for an outlay of £275,000.

Left: Memories of market shopping will be rekindled by this picture which was taken in February 1970. Market trading has been an important part of Keighley's local economy for well over 600 years. Customers have been drawn from neighbouring towns and cities to the area by the attractive stalls and reputation for unbeatable bargains generated by Keighley's traders. The Corporation regarded the market as an important element in the provision of a balanced, yet diverse range of shopping facilities for local people.

When the new market was opened in June 1971 by the Mayor, Alderman Sydney Bancroft, eager shoppers ensured record trading for the first few months. Indeed, shoppers were attracted from many other adjacent towns to experience the new market environment. It had been built at a cost of £134,000, a very modest amount by today's standards, but sufficient at the time to ensure 'state of the art' facilities. The new market was approached from Low Street, opposite Queensway and was designed with the intention of building on Keighley's long market tradition.

Bird's eye view

Showing an area of Keighley which has changed drastically in recent years, this aerial view of Hard Ings and Bradford Road was probably taken in the later 1940s to illustrate extensions to the crane works of John Smith (Keighley) Ltd. Included in the factory complex were the Mint Rock Works of manufacturing confectioners J.Bottomley and Sons Ltd., and Francis E. Cox (Keighley) Ltd., auto engineers. Today this area is dominated by the retail and leisure outlets that forms part of Keighley's 'edge-of-town' development.

Memories of Keighley

Right: A rare aerial view of the the industrial site owned by Clapham Bros. Ltd. It is thought to date from the 1930s and the railway access to the Nelson Works owned and operated by the company is clearly in shown. The rows of neatly arranged terraced housing at the top of the picture runs beside the gently sweeping curve of Lawkholme Lane. The large church at the left of the picture is Holy Trinity, noted for the controversy which was created there in the 1930s when the vicar organised Sunday dances as a ploy to boost the congregation. His scheme worked, though opinions were strongly divided as to how appropriate this was for a church organisation. Sadly the popularity of the church declined to such an extent that it was closed and demolished by the early 1970s.

Left: 1930s Keighley as seen from the new Council houses of Woodhouse. The absence of smoke suggests that this photograph was taken during a Keighley Parish Feast holiday.

There have been many changes to Keighley since this view was captured which have dramatically affected the way we travel, shop, and live. Changes which have affected our health and the way we work, with, perhaps the most drastic differences in everyday life coming in the years between 1960 and 1980. It is easy, perhaps too easy, to hark back to the 'good old days' and overlook some of the aspects of daily life which were not so pleasant. For instance, thousands of householders in 1960s Keighley still had no inside lavatory, no bathroom and no hot water supply; many houses were damp and cold in winter, health problems were more common and road deaths ran at a much higher rate than they do today. Improvements have been brought about which have changed the quality of life for ordinary folk beyond recognition.

Dixon target

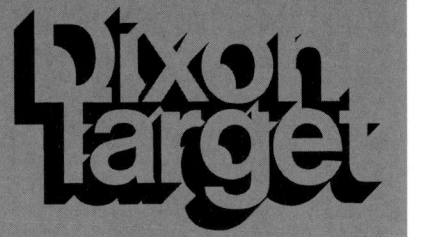

the complete print service

From Village Street Printer to Main Street Designs

Founded in the early 1900's, **Dixon Target** *became a registered limited liability company in January 1920 and so celebrated over 75 years' existence in 1995. A producer of quality letterpress, then offset, printing over all the years the company has established a tradition of customer service and attention to detail. The acquisition of Target Screen Prints of Skipton in 1982 enables the company to broaden the services it supplies to an already prestigious list of customers to include screen printing.*

The forming of **Main Street Design and Marketing** *means the company can now offer full design and marketing expertise to those customers needing printing matter, advertising and marketing support tailored to their individual style and taste.*

The clients include many nationally and internationally-known business names, organisations and charities.

Cross Hills Main Street, early 1900's

Main Street
Design & Marketing

21-25 Main Street, Cross Hills, Keighley, West Yorkshire BD20 8TX
Telephone: Cross Hills (01535) 632138 • **Sales:** (01535) 636961
Facsimile: (01535) 635983

Memories of Keighley

Reid's Bookshop, approaching a century of service to the town's booklovers

Reid's Bookshop was established in 1899 by Luther Smith. Luther was a native of Wilsden and in his earlier years had been a schoolmaster at Burnley Grammar School and then at Chippenham where he specialised in teaching art.

He first went into business as a bookseller in Bingley, establishing a small shop there until he and his family, a wife and two sons, moved to Keighley. Cavendish Street was an ideal location for a business at that time as it was one of Keighley's main thoroughfares. He bought the lease on the shop at number 10.

At that time Reids was the busiest shop in the street, housing Cavendish Street sub post office. Luther retired in 1927. A man fond of art, he spent his retirement water-colour sketching, producing works of great merit. Sadly, he died in February 1946.

Name change

After Luther's retirement in 1927 the business was purchased by JW Reid & Co and a little under a decade later it was sold to Margaret Paget. The business thrived under her care, expanding rapidly and remaining a great success. Miss Paget retired in the 1960s, when she sold the shop to Mr Mardon.

The present owners, the Brooksbanks joined the company in 1973 and the firm was incorporated, becoming Reid's Bookshop Ltd.

The move to 87 Cavendish Street

Mr Mardon retired in 1986, leaving the Brooksbanks as sole owners/directors and when the lease expired in 1995, the bookshop moved to larger premises further along at number 87 Cavendish Street.

As well as being a general bookshop, Reid's also supply books to schools and colleges and, believing that local independent shops are vital to the community, Reid's also stock a wide range of local interest books. Not bound by restrictions, Reid's can obtain any title in print in Britain.

In this fast changing time of technical advancement, books still have a vital role in education and leisure and it is a relief to realise that computers and video games have not completely taken over this new generation. There are still those around who delight in a 'good read'.

R.B.N. Cert. 4.

No. of Certificate. 414860

REGISTRATION OF BUSINESS NAMES ACT, 1916.

CERTIFICATE OF REGISTRATION.

I hereby certify that a Statement of change of particulars registered furnished by

Margaret Paget

in the business name

"J. W. Reid & Co."

of:- 8 & 10, Cavendish Street, Keighley,

pursuant to Section 6 of the above-mentioned Act was registered on the 1st day of October, 1936.

Dated this 6th day of October, 19 36.

Registrar of Business Names.

REID'S BOOKSHOP

Part of Keighley's Heritage!
Established in 1899

Part of Keighley now!
A great range of titles for pleasure and entertainment

Part of Keighley's future!
Supplier to local colleges and schools

A GOOD 'REID' FOR ALL THE FAMILY
87 Cavendish Street, Keighley.
Tel: 01535 603713 Fax: 01535 611773

Left: *This certificate was given to Margaret Paget on 6th October 1936 when she took over the business from JW Reid & Co.*

Memories of Keighley

A remarkable story of determination leading to success going back almost a hundred years

In 1899 Tom Harrison rented accommodation in the yard of the Great Northern Railway, now the site of Sainsbury's Supermarket, and began trading as a Bolt & Nut Merchant. He took consignments of fasteners straight from the train and delivered them by hand cart to the various engineering Companies in Keighley. That situation continued until 1910 when Arthur Clough formed a partnership with Tom Harrison.

New Premises

The Company was originally incorporated on the 24th September 1912 under the Companies (Consolidation) Act of 1908 and it was probably at this time that Park Royd Works, Park Street, were rented from Keighley Corporation from where the Company operated until October 1962. Tom Harrison was an engineer by trade and there is reference to a shed being erected in the yard adjacent to Park Royd Works in which a small fastener manufacturing unit was established. Tom Harrison took control of this unit while Arthur Clough ran the merchanting side.

The Oldham Bolt & Nut Works Ltd went into liquidation in 1912 and Harrison & Clough Ltd bought the plant and business, reforming it as The Oldham Bolt & Nut Works (1912) Limited. Tom Harrison took control of that Company, leaving Arthur Clough to run the merchanting side in Keighley. Communication and commuting between Keighley and Oldham would present difficulties in that era so 1914

saw the moving of the Oldham Company to Keighley. It is said by Mr John Harrison, the son of Tom, that the whole plant was transferred to Keighley in one weekend, relocated on a site on the banks of the River Worth and named Riverside Forge. The Company was renamed The Keighley Bolt & Nut Works Ltd and at this point both partners took equal shares in both businesses.

Partnership

Trade must have been good because, such was the confidence of both partners, that in 1917 they formally agreed never to dissolve their partnership. However, in 1919 Arthur Clough changed his mind and asked Tom Harrison to agree to end the partnership, to which he took strong exception. Arthur Clough's response was to threaten to start his own

First floor premises in Starkie Street - 1962 to 1968

Memories of Keighley

business in competition. Finally, they agreed to go their own separate ways, both partners buying the other out of the two businesses. Tom Harrison retained the manufacturing plant and Arthur Clough took the merchanting unit retaining the name of Harrison & Clough Ltd.

About this time Herbert Hutchinson was demobilised from the army after the First World War, only to find that his position in the Accounts Office of I & I Craven, one of the largest textile mills in the area, was no longer open to him.

After a lengthy period of unemployment, in which he did casual work for various Companies, he joined Tom Harrison at the Keighley Bolt & Nut Works as bookkeeper.

Hard times

Unfortunately, during the great recession of the 1920s the Keighley Bolt & Nut Company went into decline and was eventually sold to William Judson who changed the firm into a merchanting Company in competition with Harrison & Clough Ltd.

Again, Herbert Hutchinson was out of work but equipped with his bookkeeping experience and his new found fastener knowledge he joined Harrison & Clough Ltd., where he eventually became Sales Representative.

During the early thirties Arthur Clough became seriously ill and died about 1936 leaving all his shares to various family members. His death left the Company without Directors, with no shareholders participating. The Office Manager at that time was Mr William Henry Smith and so he and Herbert Hutchinson met the shareholders and it was agreed that controlling interest in Harrison & Clough Ltd. should pass to Messrs Smith & Hutchinson through the sale of shares to them. Mr Smith bought rather more shares that Mr Hutchinson and thus established himself as Managing Director.

Upon taking control of the business they found that the Company was virtually bankrupt. It was able to continue trading up to the Second World War when there was still a demand for bolts and nuts, although supply was very limited. That limited supply situation, together with the resultant price stability gave the Company a breathing space in which it was able to develop a lucrative export trade to India.

After the War trade continued and, in an attempt to strengthen the business, Harrison & Clough Ltd developed into a general engineer's merchant while still specialising in fasteners.

All change

In 1957 the Company was restructured, again for financial reasons, and traded for a very short time as H. & C. (Keighley) Ltd. The Company, as it now stands, was re-registered on the 1st of July 1957 again as Harrison & Clough Ltd and again with William Smith as Managing Director and Herbert Hutchinson as Sales Director, holding the same joint controlling interest as before.

In February 1962 William Smith died and it was then that Herbert Hutchinson invited his son, Neville, to join the Company.

At the time Neville Hutchinson was 27 years old and had spent 10 years in the motor vehicle repair trade. He left a junior managerial position in that trade to learn the workings of Harrison & Clough Ltd. In April of that year Henry Fewster left Keighley Boys Grammar School to join the Company, destined to become the Executive Sales Manager.

1962 was also the year that Keighley Corporation was demolishing old property in preparation for the town centre re-development. Harrison & Clough Ltd had, therefore, to vacate Park Royd Works and found temporary accommodation in Goulbourne Street, renting 7,000 sq.ft. of space above Smith & Johnson Ltd for a rent of £7.00 per week.

January 1964 saw the employment of a new office boy named David Shaw, again a school leaver destined to achieve success later in his career as General Manager. Being established in the new but temporary accommodation, with Neville Hutchinson now a Director, the prime concern was to get this small engineers merchant, with a total staff of nine and an annual turnover of £52,000, up and running and able to compete with other larger merchants in the area.

GKN

Opportunity presented itself when GKN Screws & Fasteners decided to cease trading with every ironmonger in the land and distribute its woodscrew and allied products through a hundred specially picked, nationally appointed wholesalers. Although infinitesimally small, compared with other applicants, Harrison & Clough Ltd had always fostered a very close trading relationship with GKN and it was because of that relationship and after much negotiating, mainly from the begging position on bended knee, that the Company was granted Class B distributor status and two years in which to increase its £8,000 per year spend with GKN to £50,000 per year. This was accomplished within 12 months, which GKN recognised as a sign of commitment and acknowledged by offering a distributorship for their sister Company, GKN Bolts & Nuts.

Armed with these two distributorships the Company had the key to every ironmonger's and engineer's merchant's door in the area. Because at that time there was no motorway network, larger distributors in Sheffield, Manchester and Newcastle could not deliver

Memories of Keighley

into West Yorkshire and North East Lancashire on a regular basis and so Harrison & Clough Ltd. claimed that territory as its own, saturating the area with daily and prompt deliveries.

The Company grew steadily, now working regular overtime to service customers and delivering by its own transport. With an annual turnover in 1968 of almost £208,000 it had long since outgrown its new temporary premises.

Fortunately 16,000 sq.ft. of Warehouse and Office space became available for sale further up Goulbourne Street and so again the Company removed into premises which, for the first time, it owned.

Book-keeping

By now the Company was seriously growing and the 'book-keeping' was becoming more than could be managed by the traditional 'double entry manual' system.

Enter another young man, although not a school leaver, was only 19 years old but with sound bookkeeping knowledge. He had an eye for improvement both in his career and also developing an Accounts Office in a growing business. Roy Ellison was that young man. His eminence grew with the Company and now he holds the position of Executive Accounts Manager.

At the time of Roy Ellison's employment the Company owned one *Sharp Compet* electronic calculator. Although it could only add, subtract, multiply and divide in decimals it was the size of a present-day VDU terminal. This was before decimalisation, all invoicing being in pounds, shillings and pence, so the operator had to be very mentally agile in order to convert traditional money into decimal equivalents when using the Sharp Compet. From that point onwards Roy Ellison was instrumental in establishing an Accounts Office into which was progressively introduced electronic aids and systems as they became available, culminating in the purchase of the first NCR Computer in 1978.

Established in the larger premises the Company was in a position to plan further growth and in order to accomplish that aim Neville Hutchinson was promoted to Managing Director from Joint Managing Director, a position he had coupled with Sales Director. He developed the reliable distribution of GKN products within a 50 mile radius of Keighley.

Look north

In order to develop the business further and also enable Neville Hutchinson to fulfil the role of Managing Director, a representative was employed to manage the existing customer base. Henry Fewster had been appointed buyer, thus creating the time for Neville Hutchinson to explore new sales territories. Nineteen-seventy was the year that 'Cumberland', as it was then known, was canvassed. The motorway system was still in its infancy, the M6 terminating at Lancaster.

Fastener supplies into Cumberland were on a very haphazard basis. Those suppliers involved made deliveries only when they had what they considered to be a worthwhile load. That attitude was seen as an opportunity for Harrison & Clough Ltd and it was instrumental in formulating the bedrock of the Company's future sales policy, "Offer a reliable regular delivery on the same day every week, irrespective of the volume to be delivered."

The Cumberland customers had never had such convenience and business in that area grew. Fortunately so did the motorway network with the M6 reaching Penrith and eventually Carlisle.

In 1972 the Company was again outgrowing itself and soon saw the appointment of John Dewhirst, who was recruited from Rycrofts in Bradford. John was an ironmonger by trade but had gained extensive fastener experience at Rycrofts and so was instrumental in creating a Purchasing Office and systems within Harrison & Clough Ltd, thus releasing Henry Fewster to become a representative.

The Company continued to grow, being intent on giving the most reliable delivery service in fasteners to customers. It was helped by a Keighley born Labour Chancellor of the Exchequer, Dennis Healey, whose policies encouraged high levels of stock holding. Such were the tax benefits available through annual increases in stock values that even more Warehouse space was required and 5,000 sq.ft. was rented in Thwaites Village in 1975.

Memories of Keighley

The spring of 1978 saw another 8,000 sq.ft. rented in Eastwood Mills at the end of Aireworth Road. Although it was known that the property would soon have to be demolished to make way for the Aire Valley Trunk Road, the need for Warehouse space was desperate.

Office accommodation and when completed in July 1981 the Company transferred the Goulbourne Street operation to Aireworth Road and for the first time in six years enjoyed the luxury of operating from one site.

New blood

Nineteen eighty one was also the year of major recession in which turnover fell significantly and profits substantially, but once that was over the business prospered well in the 80's. Sales turnover quadrupled, two more Warehouses were built on the Aireworth Road site and during those years Neville Hutchinson's two sons, Mark and Ian, were to leave College as graduates and join the business. After learning the trade they joined the Main Board, becoming Operations Director and Sales Director respectively.

Mark and Ian's influence brought new energy and purpose to the business. January 1994 saw the opening of a further 17,000 sq.ft. of Warehouse space on Royd Ings Avenue in which to store fasteners, and also the renting of a trunking depot in Leicester, into which consignments are delivered at 4.00am daily before being distributed in the South of England by the company's own second fleet of vehicles.

In the North the service was also extended to Glasgow and Edinburgh, business being developed to such an extent that daily deliveries are made in order to support the Scottish based representative.

In order to utilise fully the potential of two new young Directors, it was decided to extend the stock range to include hand tools. November 1994 saw the recruitment of Jeff Linley as Tool Manager. His experience and influence encouraged major tool manufacturers to give their support and in January 1995 the first small deliveries of hand tools were being made to the existing customers.

At the age of 60, in 1995, Neville Hutchinson relinquished the position of Managing Director in favour of his eldest son, Mark, Ian retaining the position of Sales Director.

Under their influence the Company has continued to grow with hand tool sales now accounting for over 20% of turnover, a remarkable achievement in little over two years. Since 1899 the story of Harrison & Clough is one of success, despite a great many obstacles. Today the firm looks forward, with a staff of 225 to the new millennium with a great deal of confidence in the knowledge that it is well placed to meet the challenges ahead.

The present day premises on Aireworth Road

Goulbourne Street premises - 1968 to 1981

Holding stock in three locations made the business very inefficient and so the search began for land on which the whole Company could eventually be relocated.

Good fortune smiled in the form of 2-9 acres being available behind Aireworth Mills and the summer of 1979 saw the first 16,000 sq.ft. of Warehouse space completed on the present site enabling both rented Warehouses to be vacated.

Building work continued on a second Warehouse and

Memories of Keighley

H. H. Calmon & Co. - a local firm with half a century of excellence in fabric manufacturing

Calmon are producers of high quality labels, tie and dress fabrics, swing tickets, packaging and identification products for the textile and clothing industry. Located in West Yorkshire, the heart of Britain's Textile Industry, a long standing history of traditional skills combined with the latest technology enables them to provide a versatile and efficient service.

HH Calmon who founded the company in 1947.

Hans Herman Calmon who founded the company in 1947 was born in Berlin of Jewish Parents on 28th September 1913, and from an early age showed a flair for design, colour and style. Small wonder that he took an interest in textiles and on leaving school, he took up a two year apprenticeship with Gebrueder Simon in Berlin. After this, he went to study at Roubaix, then the principle city of the French textile trade. Later he came to England and from a small office in the shadow of St Paul's Cathedral in London, began an import-export business with Czechoslovakia.

War interrupted his business but when normality returned to England he decided to take up a post-graduate degree at Leeds University, studying textiles. Soon, armed with his specialist knowledge he began a small business, using other people's looms to convert his ideas into fabrics which he would then sell to the one time vast Leeds tailoring industry. The first label weaving machines were purchased in 1952 when a market for garment labels was recognised as having great business potential. Growth was steady in those initial years of weaving on traditional shuttle looms. Chairman Tony Lee took over as Managing Director in the mid 1970s and 1980 saw the installation of the first broadlooms, increasing weaving capacity manyfold.

Since the mid 1980s, rapid and continuing expansion has prevailed. From 1987 to 1993, three phases of building added 35,000 square feet and 1996 saw the purchase of the former Dean Smith and Grace offices in Pitt Street only a stone's throw away from the head offices in Parkwood Street, Keighley. The weaving capacity has now reached 47 Rapier looms and 36 Needle looms.

To support the large investment in greatly increasing the volume and speed of production, computerised order tracking, stock holding, control and dispatch systems were introduced and are systematically updated in line with the growth of the company. An electronic fax system was installed in 1996 and it is now possible to receive orders direct from customers though E.D.I. (Electronic Data Interchange).

Computer Aided Design came to Calmon in 1984 and took over from the more traditional (time consuming) methods of hand painting designs on point paper. They maintain their own Creative Design Department which equally assists other customers who do not have a design facility of their own.

The Technical Design Department houses six work stations and operates on a two shift system. Here, the

Memories of Keighley

formed. It now has five looms, with more in the pipeline, a full set of back-up and design systems and a work force of 20.

In 1996 Calmon USA were created and are growing rapidly under the energetic guidance of Rob Kaliner and his team.

The company product range includes: Woven labels, printed labels, swing tickets, pocket plasters, button bags, plastic tickets, adhesive backed labels, leather patches, waist band inserts, overlooked and die-cut badges, decorative ribbon and braids, kick tapes and fancy jacquard fabrics for Ties, Waistcoats, Dress fabrics and Braces.

Facing page, left: Facing page, right: Heaton and Flint Foundry, (now demolished) on the site of the modern, purpose built Calmon factory at Parkwood Street. **Left:** *This photograph shows the workforce in January 1957. They have possibly been celebrating Christmas but nowadays their sober suits seem a little out of keeping with the decorations.*

CALMON

CREATIVE JACQUARD WEAVERS
WOVEN LABELS - PRINTED LABELS - SWING TICKETS - TIE FABRICS, FANCY JACQUARD FABRICS

HH Calmon & Co Ltd,
1 Parkwood Street, Keighley,
West Yorkshire BD21 4QR
Telephone: 01535 211211
Fax: 01535 662988

company's skilled team of designers have developed many new and exciting techniques, keeping it at the forefront of the latest Computer Aided Design Technology.

In 1989 a new 18,000 square feet building was purchased near Oporto, in Portugal and a label weaving company was established utilising the latest CAD/CAM technology with a capacity of ten electronic weaving machines. The Hong Kong warehousing facility began in 1990 in order that Calmon labels could be stocked and distributed in the Far East, especially to service UK and USA store groups. It became a wholly owned subsidiary of H.H. Calmon & Co. Ltd. in 1994 coinciding with the opening of new offices and warehousing.

The only label weaver in Ireland was purchased in 1991 and capacity is presently though nine electronic weaving machines. In 1993 a well established Printing and Packaging company based in Keighley was acquired, adding a whole new area of activity for Calmon. It now houses 33 employees and produces quality swing tickets and packaging. A joint venture was agreed with a weaver in India in 1993 and Calmon Abacus was

Memories of Keighley

Magnet, one of Keighley's best known businesses since 1919

Today Magnet is a household name, but the company can trace its roots back to 1919, when local man Tom Duxbury bought up a small timber yard. He began by buying large amounts of timber from the government and selling it on to local farmers. Originally known as The Magnet Firelighter Company, Tom bought the business for the price of his horse. In the 1920s Tom's sons, Harry Lewis and John entered the business and it was expanded to include the manufacture and sale of garages, bungalows and shops, early examples of what would later be called *pre-fabs*. Through this development joinery equipment and machinery was installed in the Bingley premises in 1924.

Trend setting company

It then became possible to make quite sophisticated joinery; door frames, windows and mouldings, as well as building timbers used by the local builders. As demand increased, more machinery was bought and Magnet Joinery, as it had been re-named, went into mass production of joinery products, a concept unknown in 1926. During that year a travelling salesman based at Birmingham was appointed but for twelve months found little trade. In 1928 he had a break through with an order to supply components for 500 houses to be built for the Birmingham Corporation. An influx of orders followed from all over England, including 150 houses in Manchester, 600 in Leeds and 300 in Wolverhampton. This meant that a new plant was needed and during the winter of 1929 the Bingley factory was expanded.

Phoenix from the ashes

On the night of February 28th 1929 a serious fire occurred which destroyed most of the factory and machinery. This tragedy didn't deter the directors, who as soon as the fire was put out, began to rebuild the factory out of the ashes. Superhuman effort and a willing workforce led to a portion of the factory being back in production just six weeks later. Only one contract (the Manchester housing contract for 150 houses) was lost.

Magnet go public

In 1936 Magnet Joinery formed a Public Limited Company with a capital of £120,000 and the following year, a subsidiary, Magnet Timber Ltd was formed. It was based at Grays in Essex, producing moulded woodwork, standard doors and joinery. Throughout the war years Magnet was engaged in the war effort, and Magnet Timber produced doors for the Ministry of Works. Prior to the outbreak of war the company was distributing its products throughout England. In 1942 Magnet Joinery Ltd acquired a sawmilling business in Knaresborough, and from that year the company was able to cut out the middle man, using wood produced by the sawmilling division for use in its other concerns.

Keighley

Production was centralised in 1965 a 42 acre site in Keighley. A subsidiary

Memories of Keighley

company, William Browns Sawmills Ltd at Darlington manufactured kitchen units, stairs and specialist joinery, supplying the branches in Birmingham, Liverpool, Bingley and other towns across the country.

Merger with Southern-Evans

In 1975 Magnet merged with Southern-Evans Ltd, by which time Magnet had become Britain's leading supplier of doors, windows and other joinery products. Southern-Evans formed in 1968 when Southerns Ltd (a company founded over a century earlier) and William Evans (founded in 1902) were merged. After the merger with William Evans, Southern-Evans was considered to be one of the foremost groups in the UK timber industry. Importing hardwoods, softwoods and sheet materials through 80 branches countrywide, it became clear why the merger with Magnet was beneficial.

Both companies combined, producing kitchen units, stairs and joinery from many types of wood made the newly formed company one of the most powerful in the home improvement industry.

Diversity

At a time when the home building market was flat, restoration, renovation and home improvements were areas of great activity. The Magnet & Southerns Group had over 260 outlets and were in a strong position to serve this market. Most branches had bright, modern showrooms where products could be shown off in real-life settings.

the group was split, to provide service both to retail and trade customers.

Today

The company is now owned by Berisford International PLC and also has factories in Darlington, Rotherham, Flint and Penrith with 213 branches and showrooms nationwide. What began as a small local concern just after the end of the great war has now grown to be a major national business, but is very proud to retain its Keighley roots

Success

Since the merger the company has been highly successful, despite the depressed state of the building trade. Magnet now offers a complete service to consumers, builders, joiners, property repairers and home handymen.

Management buyout

In October 1988 Magnet sold off their Southerns-Evans outlets to Harcros Timber and Building Supplies in an attempt to prepare for management buyout which went ahead in 1989. By November of that year, the company finances had been restructured and Mr John Foulkes had been brought in as Group Managing Director. The long reigning Chairman, Mr JT Duxbury (a descendent of the founder) resigned in January 1990 and Mr Foulkes was appointed Group Chairman. The following month

Above: One of the extensive ranges of kitchen furniture available from Magnet. *Facing page:* This photograph dates from around the 1930s and shows *Head Mill, Whitley Street, Bingley.* *Above left:* Another 1930s photograph shows three lorries loaded with staircases and windows ready for delivery.

Magnet

Magnet Limited,
Royd Ings Avenue,
Keighley, West Yorkshire
BD21 4BY
Telephone: 01535 661133

Memories of Keighley

Oakbank School - a proud history of success and achievement

At the beginning of the seventeenth century Keighley Free Grammar School was established as a result of legacies granted by John Drake (1713), an innkeeper and maltster of Church Green and by Jonas Tonson of Exley (1716 and 1718). At that time and for 250 years afterwards the school was located in the centre of Keighley. The Drake & Tonson Trust still operates and provides the school with about £6,000 per year.

This Free Grammar School developed into two schools - Keighley Girls' Grammar (subsequently Greenhead School) and Keighley Boys' Grammar (subsequently Oakbank School).

The Boys' Grammar School moved to its present site in 1964, It was constructed around the solid Victorian house built in 1872 by John Haggas, a worsted manufacturer. From here, over his large estates on which he bred cattle, he could overlook his mills at Ingrow. At Christmas the choir of the local church used to sing carols in the hallway of the house. The fine balcony was often covered with soaked riding gear as the Haggas daughters, Daisy and Gladys returned from a day's riding at Boston Spa.

During the war the house was occupied by several evacuated families. In 1946 it was purchased with the estates for £15,000 by Keighley Borough Council. It then became the Keighley Remedial Centre, providing small group work in basic subjects for those children who had been absent from school for long periods of time due to long illnesses. In 1964 a new Keighley School was opened on the site which later became known as Oakbank School, but which was originally named Keighley Boys' Grammar

Memories of Keighley

OAKBANK SCHOOL
Centre of Sporting excellence

**OAKWORTH ROAD, KEIGHLEY,
WEST YORKSHIRE BD22 7DU**

Headteacher: Mr John Roberts BA
Telephone: 01535 662787 Fax: 01535 691045

We are proud of our sporting achievement. Last year Oakbank had 43 pupils representing Bradford, West Yorkshire and England and has won ten Bradford Championships over a range of sports.

At Oakbank we are equally proud of our increased academic performance and provision:
- An increase in the proportion of students gaining 5 A-C GCSE grades by 50%
- Out of all the Bradford schools we had the second highest A Level result
- Last summer we invested £150,000 in new classrooms and facilities with more planned this year
- A sixth form of 220 students in its own centre and with its own study facilities. This year it has attracted students from schools in North Yorkshire, Bradford and Calderdale
- A wide range of GNVQ courses at 14+ and 16+
- Working in partnership with business and industry to provide work experience for over 300 youngsters per year
- And now a government maintained sports college

All in all, a school to be proud of!

OAKBANK SCHOOL - FOUNDED 1713
INCORPORATED AS A GRANT MAINTAINED SCHOOL IN 1993

Winners of awards since 1988 from:
Creativity in Science and Technology; Micro-electronic Support Unit
National Centre for Electronics and Technology; Leadership1990
National Centre for the Study of Comprehensive Schools
Institute for Education in International Understanding
European Year of the Environment; Flexible Learning Project
Avista (School Marketing National Award)
Royal Anniversary Trust's School Award

In 1967, along with most schools in the country at around this time, the Grammar School became a comprehensive. This was a turbulent time for the school as teachers suddenly had to cope with pupils other than the selected academic high fliers. Another momentous change came when the school became co-educational and settled down to become a 13-18 school in the three tier system of first, middle and upper schools.

In 1993 the school opted out of the control of Bradford local education authority when it became grant maintained. It is still funded by the state but is governed with complete independence by its governing body. In 1997 Oakbank gained the status of a specialist Sports College, one of only six in the country.

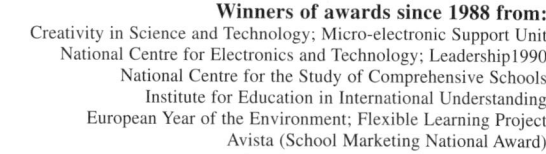

Today, the pupils, parents and staff of Oakbank School can feel justifiably proud of academic results that are a match for the best schools in the Bradford district, and sporting achievements that are unequalled in the area.

Above: An early prize evening. Facing page: Early days at the school camp in Kirkcudbright.

Keighley College

Cavendish Street, Keighley, West Yorkshire BD21 3DF

Serving the community for more than 150 years

WORKING DAY and NIGHT FOR YOUR SUCCESS

1000s of training opportunities
Don't miss yours - apply now

Whether you are a school leaver or mature student planning a new career or someone looking to advance a career we can help you attain your goal.

Many courses are linked to school times, others have day or evening options and if you are unemployed you can study on many of the courses without loss of benefit.

For information about enrolment details and our wide range of courses contact the Guidance Centre on

(01535) 618600

Delivering quality training to the community

Memories of Keighley

Joseph Ogden Ltd, five generations of progress and still growing

Today, Joseph Ogden Ltd is a well known local business employing many people. But the firm has more humble roots when it was established in 1878 by Joseph Ogden, who gained his experience in the wool trade by selling cloth to local businesses. The company description at that time was 'Wool Sorters and Staplers'. Originally based in Haworth, the firm moved to Oxenhope in the early 1880s.

Joseph Ogden Ltd is now in its fifth generation of being run by the same family, no mean feat by anybody's standards. Joseph had two sons; Joseph Zera and George. Joseph Zera went into his own business whilst George, the elder of Joseph's sons, left school in the early 1900s and went straight into the family business. When he inherited the business he moved it to Perseverance Mills, installing wool combing machinery to allow for diversification. The company remained here for about fifty years. George's son, Herbert took over in the mid 1930s and ran the business through the war, when most of Britain saw shortages in raw materials and personnel.

Business was slow but steady and although the company didn't see much profit at the time, it survived. Herbert ran the mill (producing wool for the war wool commission)

Springhead Mills in Keighley, which has been the home of Joseph Ogden since 1985.

with an ARP watch station operating from his office. Herbert remained in control until 1960 when his son took over. Chris Ogden removed the wool combing machinery and ran the company from an office, on his own, producing synthetic fibre tops made on commission.

Expansion soon became necessary due to an influx of orders and premises were found at Vale Mills, Oakworth. The move took place in 1970 and the company remained here until 1985 when it finally moved to Springhead Mills.

The company has seen many challenges and overcome more obstacles along the way, not least of which was the difficulty in obtaining raw materials at certain times, especially during both wars.

The textile industry has always had a tenuous hold on life. Joseph Ogden Ltd has combated this to some extent by producing their own machinery, (there has, however been an ulcer or two along the way!) But despite all this, the company remains resolute in its aims to expand. Today, the company produces yarn for socks, textiles for wool blends and fibres for industrial uses such as car batteries, threads, ropes and filters. The company's main customers are the textile hosiery industry and the automotive industry, where the company prides itself on its ability to find a niche in any market. "If nobody else makes it - we will!"

There is also a certain amount of pride in its recycling capabilities. If a type of fibre can only be used in two or three products, the company takes the waste and puts it into a further product that other companies don't make. Joseph Ogden Ltd has a history as diverse as any novel. It has witnessed many changes in England and overcome anything that got in its way. Sheer hard work and commitment to the cause have led Joseph Ogden Ltd to become the company it is today, and it is these aims that will lead it into the millennium and beyond.

Memories of Keighley

Local firm that survived two world wars prospers into next century

The Atkinson Dyeing company originally belonged to Herbert Roberts Co Ltd, which has since moved to Beechcliffe. Walter Atkinson bought the property and the equipment in 1907 and started his business of cotton warp dyers, winders and ballers. Walter ran the business through the first three decades of this century, expanding despite the First World War and the ensuing depression until his son (also called Walter) took over in the late 1930s.

The war years were tough for the firm. Requisitioned by the War Office to produce yarn for the war effort the company also lost most of its workforce as its employees went off to serve in the forces. Despite these struggles the spirit of the company prevailed and it survived the war. Sadly Walter died soon afterwards and the business was purchased by Clifford Pickles, who had worked for the founder as a lorry driver. He became the managing director until his retirement in 1970 when Walter Young, who was the grandson of the founder took over the reins, with John Roberts becoming chairman. John Roberts had previously been a director under Clifford Pickles' management. Walter Young ran the business until 1986 when he sold it to the Wolstenholme family. Walter died on March 6th 1997.

Neil Wolstenholme has now taken full control of the company, taking over the reins from his father, Harry. Neil had been given management experience by previously running a commission beaming and winding business in Halifax, Browbridge Textiles. This business moved from Halifax and now occupies the same premises as Atkinson Dyeing, the purpose being to streamline and economise both businesses. Browbridge is now the parent company of Atkinson Dyeing Company, with the same board of directors and Neil as managing director of both.

The company specialised in cross ball cotton yarn dyeing and is the only Yorkshire company to do this process, used in the manufacture of Moquettes. The company is also the main supplier to John Holdsworth in Halifax, whose business is the world leader in the manufacture of fabrics for the transport industry.

The company has now moved into dyeing yarn on packages and has invested heavily in new plant and machinery which will enable it to meet future demand over the coming years.

Top left: *Walter Young who ran the company until his retirement in 1986.*
Right: *The old cross ball dyeing range.*

Memories of Keighley

Centenary nears for Keighley Library

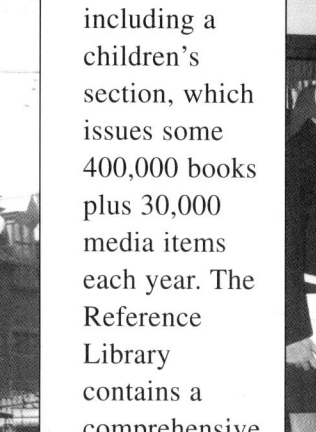

Keighley Library is a Grade II listed building and is one of the most remarkable public buildings in the North of England. It was the first Public Library in England to be funded by Andrew Carnegie the American manufacturer and philanthropist, a fact of which the people of Keighley should be justifiably proud.

The building opened to the public in 1904, having been designed by McKewan and Swan of Birmingham. Alterations done to the original building over the years have included an extension added in 1961 which provided a Children's Library and First Floor Lecture Hall. The Children's Library was incorporated into the main Lending Library in the 1980s in order to improve the service to children. This area then became the Education Library Service for teachers, but is now occupied by Keighley Citizen's Advice Bureau.

The Library operates as part of the City of Bradford Metropolitan District Council Library network and is a popular and well used facility, with some 450,000 people of all ages coming through the doors each year. The Library has a well used lending collection including a children's section, which issues some 400,000 books plus 30,000 media items each year. The Reference Library contains a comprehensive and up-to-date collection of business and career information and extensive and well-used study facilities.

It also houses a remarkable local history and archive collection relating to the town and local area. The Lecture Hall provides much needed facilities for a wide range of community groups.

In addition, the Library provides a wide range of information, including Council information and Government information, current events and Open Learning material.

For your Books, Media, Information, Reference and study facilities
Keighley Library, North Street, Keighley BD21 3SX
Telephone: 01535 618212

Opening hours:
Monday and Wednesday: 9.00am - 7.00pm
Tuesday: 9.00am - 1.00pm
Thursday: 9.30am - 7.00pm
Friday and Saturday: 9.00am - 5.00pm

City of BRADFORD METROPOLITAN DISTRICT COUNCIL

Memories of Keighley

Keighley Business Forum – building on Keighley's proud past

The early nineteenth century completion of the Leeds & Liverpool Canal along the valley of the River Aire emphasised the importance of this relatively low trans-Pennine route between the West Riding and Lancashire and it seems obvious that the ments were evident along the route in Bingley and Keighley was then in the process of being transformed from an old fashioned village into a flourishing town. Low Mill had already been erected in the water meadows by the River Worth in 1780 and further develop-Skipton. This provided a strong case for extending the line at least to Keighley and the decision was soon taken to go beyond there, to Skipton and Colne.

The line was laid as far as Keighley by early 1847, despite difficulties laying the lines over the Bingley Bog! The route was considered safe and the line was opened to the public, who turned out in their droves on Tuesday 16th March 1847. Keighley had indeed been transformed!

early railway engineers would choose to follow the same route. The line, popularly known as 'The Airedale Line', was constructed and opened to public passenger transport in three stages.

Early transformation

The lower Aire was first seen by the newly formed Leeds and Bradford Railway Company merely as a means of providing a level, if indirect route through Shipley between Leeds (Wellington) and Bradford (Market Street) and it was formally opened on 30th June 1846. This provided an opportunity for developments North Westwards along the Aire Valley which was by that time already partly industrialised.

The Keighley Business Forum

The Keighley Business Forum was established in 1989 as a result of several local businesses taking their futures into their own hands through self-help initiative. The KBF aim was then, and still is, to regenerate the local economy, improve business performance, attract inward investment and foster job creation. Like their forward thinking ancestors who saw the railways as a means to expand, the KBF see their services as a way of promoting business in the area. Many local businesses have benefited from the KBF and the partnerships formed with specialist outside agencies and institutions. All work together with considerable success for the same common goal the present and future well-being of the area, its companies and communities.

Above: Keighley Business Forum staff at a recent Keighley 150th anniversary celebrations. **Left:** KBF Director Ian Copping with representatives from different organisations who visited Keighley to see how the Forum works. **Above left:** Keighley Station as seen in 1847.